NorthStar 3
READING & WRITING
FOURTH EDITION

Authors   LAURIE BARTON

              CAROLYN DUPAQUIER

Series Editors   FRANCES BOYD

              CAROL NUMRICH

D1275206

Dedication

I would like to dedicate this edition
to my husband, Craig, and to my
children, Jonathan and Annalise.
Without their love and support, I
could not have completed this book.
Laurie Barton

To my husband, Luis, and to
my children, Alexander and Alyse,
who let me work.
Carolyn Dupaquier Sardinas

NorthStar: Reading & Writing Level 3, Fourth Edition

Copyright © 2015, 2009, 2004, 1998 by Pearson Education, Inc.
All rights reserved.

No part of this publication may be reproduced, stored in a retrieval system, or transmitted in any
form or by any means, electronic, mechanical, photocopying, recording, or otherwise, without the
prior permission of the publisher.

Pearson Education, 10 Bank Street, White Plains, NY 10606

Contributor credit: Cynthia Boardman

Staff credits: The people who made up the **NorthStar: Reading & Writing Level 3, Fourth Edition** team,
representing editorial, production, design, and manufacturing, are Kimberly Casey, Tracey Cataldo,
Rosa Chapinal, Aerin Csigay, Mindy DePalma, Dave Dickey, Niki Lee, Françoise Leffler, Amy McCormick,
Mary Perrotta Rich, Robert Ruvo, Christopher Siley, and Debbie Sistino

Text composition: ElectraGraphics, Inc.
Editorial services: Wildwood Ink

Library of Congress Cataloging-in-Publication Data

Haugnes, Natasha, 1965–
  Northstar 2 : Reading and writing / Authors: Natasha Haugnes, Beth Maher. — Fourth Edition.
    pages cm
  ISBN-13: 978-0-13-338216-7 (Level 2) – ISBN 978-0-13-294039-9 (Level 3) – ISBN 978-0-13-338223-5
(Level 4) – ISBN 978-0-13-338224-2 (Level 5)
1. English language—Textbooks for foreign speakers. 2. Reading comprehension—Problems,
exercises, etc. 3. Report writing—Problems, exercises, etc. I. Maher, Beth, 1965- II. Title. III.
Title: Northstar two. IV. Title: Reading and writing.
  PE1128.H394 2015
  428.2'4—dc23
                                                                              2013050584

ISBN 10: 0-13-294039-6
ISBN 13: 978-0-13-294039-9

Printed in the United States of America
1 2 3 4 5 6 7 8 9 10—V057—20 19 18 17 16 15 14

CONTENTS

WELCOME TO

NORTHSTAR

A BLENDED-LEARNING COURSE FOR THE 21ST CENTURY

Building on the success of previous editions, *NorthStar* continues to engage and motivate students through new and updated contemporary, authentic topics in a seamless integration of print and online content. Students will achieve their academic as well as language and personal goals in order to meet the challenges of the 21st century.

New for the FOURTH EDITION

★ **Fully Blended MyEnglishLab**
NorthStar aims to prepare students for academic success and digital literacy with its fully blended online lab. The innovative new MyEnglishLab: *NorthStar* gives learners immediate feedback—anytime, anywhere—as they complete auto-graded language activities online.

★ **NEW and UPDATED THEMES**
Current and thought-provoking topics presented in a variety of genres promote intellectual stimulation. The authentic content engages students, links them to language use outside of the classroom, and encourages personal expression and critical thinking.

★ **EXPLICIT SKILL INSTRUCTION and PRACTICE**
Language skills are highlighted in each unit, providing students with systematic and multiple exposures to language forms and structures in a variety of contexts. Concise presentations and targeted practice in print and online prepare students for academic success.

★ **LEARNING OUTCOMES and ASSESSMENT**
A variety of assessment tools, including online diagnostic, formative and summative assessments, and a flexible gradebook, aligned with clearly identified unit learning outcomes, allow teachers to individualize instruction and track student progress.

THE NORTHSTAR APPROACH TO CRITICAL THINKING

What is critical thinking?

Most textbooks include interesting questions for students to discuss and tasks for students to engage in to develop language skills. Often these questions and tasks are labeled critical thinking. Look at this question as an example:

When you buy fruits and vegetables, do you usually look for the cheapest price? Explain.

The question may inspire a lively discussion with students exploring a variety of viewpoints—but it doesn't necessarily develop critical thinking. Now look at another example:

When people in your neighborhood buy fruits and vegetables, what factors are the most important: the price, the freshness, locally grown, organic (without chemicals)? Make a prediction and explain. How can you find out if your prediction is correct? This question does develop critical thinking. It asks students to make predictions, formulate a hypothesis, and draw a conclusion—all higher-level critical thinking skills. Critical thinking, as philosophers and psychologists suggest, is a sharpening and a broadening of the mind. A critical thinker engages in true problem solving, connects information in novel ways, and challenges assumptions. A critical thinker is a skillful, responsible thinker who is open-minded and has the ability to evaluate information based on evidence. Ultimately, through this process of critical thinking, students are better able to decide what to think, what to say, or what to do.

How do we teach critical thinking?

It is not enough to teach "about" critical thinking. Teaching the theory of critical thinking will not produce critical thinkers. Additionally, it is not enough to simply expose students to good examples of critical thinking without explanation or explicit practice and hope our students will learn by imitation.

Students need to engage in specially designed exercises that aim to improve critical thinking skills. This approach practices skills both implicitly and explicitly and is embedded in thought-provoking content. Some strategies include:

- subject matter that is carefully selected and exploited so that students learn new concepts and encounter new perspectives.
- students identifying their own assumptions about the world and later challenging them.
- activities that are designed in a way that students answer questions and complete language-learning tasks that may not have black-and-white answers. (Finding THE answer is often less valuable than the process by which answers are derived.)
- activities that engage students in logical thinking, where they support their reasoning and resolve differences with their peers.

Infused throughout each unit of each book, *NorthStar* uses the principles and strategies outlined above, including:

- Make Inferences: inference comprehension questions in every unit
- Vocabulary and Comprehension: categorization activities
- Vocabulary and Synthesize: relationship analyses (analogies); comparisons (Venn diagrams)
- Synthesize: synthesis of information from two texts teaches a "multiplicity" approach rather than a "duality" approach to learning; ideas that seem to be in opposition on the surface may actually intersect and reinforce each other
- Focus on the Topic and Preview: identifying assumptions, recognizing attitudes and values, and then re-evaluating them
- Focus on Writing/Speaking: reasoning and argumentation
- Unit Project: judgment; choosing factual, unbiased information for research projects
- Focus on Writing/Speaking and Express Opinions: decision making; proposing solutions

THE NORTHSTAR UNIT

1 FOCUS ON THE TOPIC

*CT Each unit begins with a photo that draws students into the topic. Focus questions motivate students and encourage them to make personal connections. Students make inferences about and predict the content of the unit.

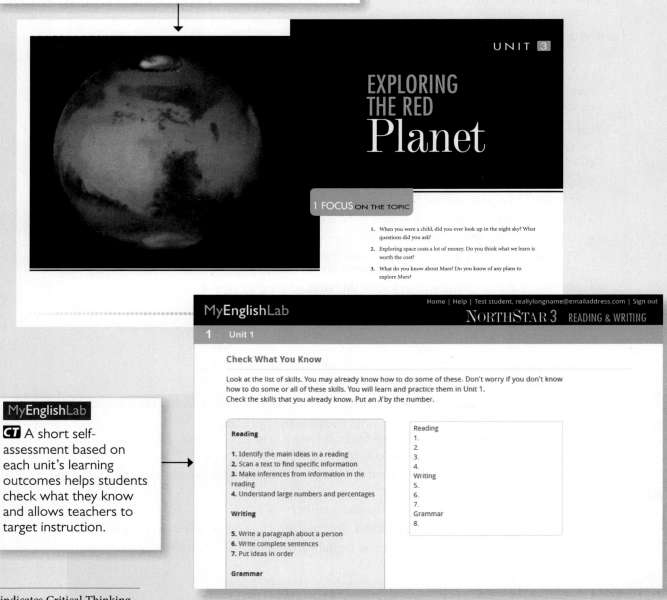

UNIT 3

EXPLORING
THE RED
Planet

1 FOCUS ON THE TOPIC

1. When you were a child, did you ever look up in the night sky? What questions did you ask?

2. Exploring space costs a lot of money. Do you think what we learn is worth the cost?

3. What do you know about Mars? Do you know of any plans to explore Mars?

Home | Help | Test student, reallylongname@emailaddress.com | Sign out

NORTHSTAR 3 READING & WRITING

MyEnglishLab

1 Unit 1

Check What You Know

Look at the list of skills. You may already know how to do some of these. Don't worry if you don't know how to do some or all of these skills. You will learn and practice them in Unit 1.
Check the skills that you already know. Put an *X* by the number.

Reading

1. Identify the main ideas in a reading
2. Scan a text to find specific information
3. Make inferences from information in the reading
4. Understand large numbers and percentages

Writing

5. Write a paragraph about a person
6. Write complete sentences
7. Put ideas in order

Grammar

Reading
1.
2.
3.
4.
Writing
5.
6.
7.
Grammar
8.

MyEnglishLab

CT A short self-assessment based on each unit's learning outcomes helps students check what they know and allows teachers to target instruction.

*indicates Critical Thinking

Two contrasting, thought-provoking readings, from a variety of authentic genres, stimulate students intellectually.

CT Students predict content, verify their predictions, and follow up with a variety of tasks that ensure comprehension.

MARS: OUR NEW HOME?

1 If you think you'd like to live on Mars, you may have that possibility by 2023. A Dutch company called Mars One will soon advertise for people interested in colonizing[1] Mars. If you have all the necessary skills—and there are a lot—you could be one of the first colonists to Mars. Are you ready for the challenge?

2 Luckily, you won't have to find the money to pay for a mission to Mars because it would cost billions of dollars. Mars One has already received money from companies and some private donors.[2] It is also **counting on** getting money from everyday people who become interested in the television show they are planning to start soon. The show will follow teams of four applicants as they complete difficult jobs in difficult situations. The audience will [...] This show will [...] television and on [...] hoping that peop [...]

in the mission that they will give small and large amounts of money. Or at least buy a t-shirt—which Mars One already has available on its website.

3 As a future colonist in one of the six teams, you will go through years of training. If your

[1] **colonize:** to control an a[...]
[2] **donor:** someone who giv[...]

Timeline for a Mission to Mars

NASA currently has three spaceships orbiting[1] Mars and three rovers and one science lab on the planet, but they don't have plans to send colonists there like Mars One does. Sending anyone—colonists for the rest of their lives or astronauts for two months—to Mars takes a lot of planning. Space researchers have suggested plans for sending people to Mars, and their plans are based on real facts. But since no

one has ever gone to Mars, their plans are only **speculations**. For example, the people at TV's Discovery Channel made a movie called *Race to Mars*, which follows a realistic timeline. The magazine *Popular Science* has also written about the steps needed to go to Mars. What timeline events can scientists agree on? Here is a plan that might be proposed.

Days 1–97 Launching[2] Spaceships
Parts for the three supply ships and one passenger ship are launched and begin to orbit the Earth. Spaceship builders put the ships together. After that, the three supply ships leave for Mars. The passenger ship waits in orbit until the astronauts arrive.

Days 98–112 Checking the Health of the Astronauts
The astronauts stay away from other people for two weeks before leaving Earth to avoid getting sick. Doctors make sure they are in good health.

---

2 Work with a partner. Scan Reading Two for the answers to these questions. Refer to the paragraphs or day numbers in parentheses.

1. How many NASA rovers are on Mars? How many ships orbit the planet? *(paragraph 1)*
2. What is *Popular Science*? *(paragraph 1)*
3. How many supply ships are necessary for a mission to Mars? *(Days 1–90)*
4. How long do the astronauts have to stay away from people before they leave for Mars? *(Days 98–112)*
5. How many days does it take to reach Mars? *(Days 116–356)*

GO TO MyEnglishLab FOR MORE SKILL PRACTICE.

CONNECT THE READINGS

STEP 1: Organize

Reading One **(R1)** and Reading Two **(R2)** contain information about Mars missions. Using this information, fill in the missing information in the chart. If there isn't a solution offered in Reading Two for a problem from Reading One, leave the cell blank.

PROBLEM (R1)	SOLUTION (R2)
1. Lack of oxygen in Mars atmosphere	Artificial habitat where oxygen in air is regulated
2. Poor soil on Mars	
3. Weak muscles, bones, and heart without gravity	
4. Feelings of isolation from home	
5. Boredom	
6.	Keeping busy with activity cause tiredness and sleep
7.	Required exercise periods

STEP 2: Synthesize

Imagine an informational interview between a Mars One representative and a woman interested in going to Mars as a colonist. Fill in the missing parts with information from the chart in Step 1.

MARS ONE: What questions do you have?

WOMAN: I've heard that the absence of gravity can cause physical problems. What kinds of physical problems?

60 UNIT 3

CT Students are challenged to take what they have learned and organize, integrate, and synthesize the information in a meaningful way.

MyEnglishLab

Auto-graded vocabulary practice activities reinforce meaning and pronunciation.

MyEnglishLab Home | Help | Test student, reallylongname@emailaddress.com | Sign out

NORTHSTAR 3 READING & WRITING

1 Unit 1

Vocabulary Practice

Match each word to a word with an opposite meaning.

artificial	ignore
boredom	surrounded
count on	doubt
depression	stimulation
isolated	perish
react	natural
spin	happiness
survive	remain still

Submit

Copyright © 2013 Pearson Education Limited | Pearson Education | www.myenglishlab.com | Terms and conditions | Cookie policy | Credits

ALWAYS LEARNING   PEARSON

EXPLICIT SKILL INSTRUCTION AND PRACTICE

CT Step-by-step instructions and practice guide students to exercise critical thinking and to dig deeper by asking questions that move beyond the literal meaning of the text.

MAKE INFERENCES

INFERRING DEGREE OF DIFFICULTY

An **inference** is an **educated guess** about something that is **not directly stated** in a text. Writers sometimes **suggest degrees of difficulty** without stating them explicitly. A strong reader can **infer** these **degrees of difficulty** by reading the text closely.

Look at the example and read the explanation.

• Considering the cost of the mission to Mars, how difficult will it be for people to join?

Circle the best answer.

a. not so difficult
b. somewhat difficult
c. difficult
d. very difficult

(The best answer is a.)

In **paragraph 2**, we learn that colonists will not have to pay for their trip. Companies and private donors will supply the money for this mission.

After reading the text closely, we can **infer** that in terms of cost, joining the mission **won't be so difficult** since people won't have to pay anything.

Circle the best answer for each of the challenges the colonists will face in the Mars mission. Refer to the paragraphs in parentheses.

1. How difficult will it be to create an artificial environment? *(paragraph 3)*

   ...lt
   ...fficult

   ...ill it be to live without or with low gravity? *(paragraph 4)*

   ...lt
   ...fficult

   (continued on next page)

COMPREHENSION

Answer the questions. Discuss your answers with a partner.

1. How long are astronauts isolated from other people before they leave Earth? Why are they isolated?
2. On Day 116, why are the engines fired?
3. How is gravity made in space, where there is no gravity?
4. Which ship(s) arrive first at Mars? Why?
5. How many work hours are there in the daily schedule during the trip to Mars?

---------- GO TO MyEnglishLab *FOR MORE VOCABULARY PRACTICE.*

READING SKILL

1 Look at Reading Two again. When you looked for the boldfaced words, did you read quickly or carefully?

SCANNING FOR DETAILS

Scanning is a useful skill that allows you to **find information quickly** without having to read the entire text. Before you carefully read Reading Two, you were asked to look at the boldfaced words. That was scanning.

In addition to **highlighted words**, you can scan for **key words, names,** or **numbers.** Key words are words that are often repeated. Look for capital letters when you want to find a name. Numbers are easy to find.

Scanning is very **useful when taking tests,** too. First read the question, and then scan the reading for the answer.

QUESTION: How many points are listed on this timeline?
  (SCAN: Count the number of underlined subheadings in the reading.)

  ANSWER: 10

QUESTION: Who made the movie *Race to Mars*?
  (SCAN: Find the title of the movie in italics and read around it.)

  ANSWER: The Discovery Channel

QUESTION: What happens on Day 417?
  (SCAN: Find that number on the list and just read what happens that day).

  ANSWER: The astronauts leave Mars.

Explicit skill presentation and practice lead to student mastery and success in an academic environment.

MyEnglishLab

Key reading skills are reinforced and practiced in new contexts. Meaningful and instant feedback provide students and teachers with essential information to monitor progress.

MyEnglishLab

Home | Help | Test student, reallylongname@emailaddress.com | Sign out

NORTHSTAR 3   READING & WRITING

1   Unit 1

Reading Skill: Scanning for Details

Look at the phrases in the left column. Scan the passage below to match each phrase to a detail in the right column.

Bas Lansdorp is a Dutch engineer who founded the company Mars One. He is confident that colonies can be built on Mars using today's technology. He says that these colonies will be similar to research stations used by scientists living in the Arctic. Mars One will train the colonists in building, growing their own food, and taking care of medical needs. The company expects over one million people to apply for the chance to travel one-way to Mars. It will cost approximately six billion dollars to finance the project, and Lansdorp believes this money can be raised through the creation of a Mars One television show.

(Source: Waldron, Ben. "Company Offers One Way Trip to Mars." abcnews.go.com)

nationality of Mars One founder	growing food
part of Mars One training	six billion
number of applicants	one-way
type of trip	over one million
cost of project in dollars	Dutch

Productive vocabulary targeted in the unit is reviewed, expanded upon, and used creatively in this section and in the final writing task. Grammar structures useful for the final writing task are presented and practiced. A concise grammar skills box serves as an excellent reference.

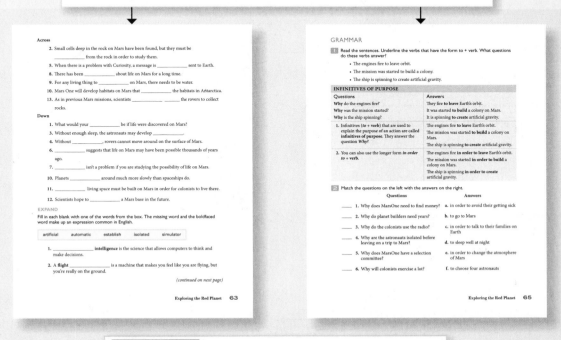

MyEnglishLab

Auto-graded vocabulary and grammar practice activities with feedback reinforce meaning, form, and function.

A TASK-BASED APPROACH TO PROCESS WRITING

3 Combine the questions and answers (from the previous activity) to make sentences that answer the questions "Why?"

1. _____ *MarsOne needs to find money to go to Mars.* _____
2. _____
3. _____
4. _____
5. _____
6. _____

GO TO MyEnglishLab FOR MORE GRAMMAR PRACTICE AND TO CHECK WHAT YOU LEARNED.

FINAL WRITING TASK

In this unit, you read about a plan to build a colony on Mars. The job of colonist is open to anyone. Would you go on a Mars mission?

You are going to *write a paragraph answering this question and explaining your decision*. What are the pros and cons of deciding one way or the other? Evaluate your own abilities. Use the vocabulary and the grammar from this unit.*

PREPARE TO WRITE: Evaluating Pros and Cons

Fill in the chart with the pros and cons of going to Mars. Don't think too much. Just list any ideas that come into your mind.

PROS	CONS

* For Alternative Writing Topics, see page 72. These topics can be used in place of the writing topic for this unit or as homework. The alternative topics relate to the theme of the unit but may not target the same grammar or rhetorical structures taught in the unit.

CT A final writing task gives students an opportunity to integrate ideas, vocabulary, and grammar presented in the unit.

CT Students organize their ideas for writing using a particular structural or rhetorical pattern.

WRITE: A Paragraph Outline

An **outline** is a plan for how you will write a text. The following outline is for writing a **paragraph**. Use outlines to help organize the main idea and details that you want to include. Use your outline to organize your topic sentence, supporting points, supporting details, and concluding sentence.

> I.   **Topic Sentence**
> II. **Supporting Point**
>   A. Supporting Detail
>   B. Supporting Detail
> III. **Supporting Point**
>   A. Supporting Detail
>   B. Supporting Detail
> IV. **Concluding Sentence**

1 Read this paragraph about a difficult decision. Then discuss the questions with a partner.

Which Mars Team Job to Take

After graduating, I chose a job at the Ames Research Center in Mountain View (near San Francisco) instead of the job at Jet Propulsion Laboratory in Pasadena (near Los Angeles) for three reasons. The first reason was emotional. Everyone in my family lives on the peninsula between San Francisco and San Jose, and I like to attend all the family get-togethers. And if I need help, I can count on them to help me. Moreover, my parents are both in their 70s, and I want to be able to help them as they get even older. Secondly, it is smoggy and hot in southern California, especially in the summer. I know this is true because I lived there for over 10 years. It is true that the air quality has improved a lot in the last 20 years, but it's not as good as the air in the Bay Area. The last reason I chose the job in northern California is that San Francisco has far fewer people than Los Angeles does. San Francisco's population is about 800,000, and Los Angeles' is about 3,500,000. San Francisco can't really grow because it is surrounded by water on three sides, but

(continued on next page)

Exploring the Red Planet   67

MyEnglishLab   Home | Help | Test student, reallylongname@emailaddress.com | Sign out
NORTHSTAR 3   READING & WRITING
1   Unit 1

Reading Skill: Scanning for Details

Look at the phrases in the left column. Scan the passage below to match each phrase to a detail in the right column.

Bas Lansdorp is a Dutch engineer who founded the company Mars One. He is confident that colonies can be built on Mars using today's technology. He says that these colonies will be similar to research stations used by scientists living in the Arctic. Mars One will train the colonists in building, growing their own food, and taking care of medical needs. The company expects over one million people to apply for the chance to travel one-way to Mars. It will cost approximately six billion dollars to finance the project, and Lansdorp believes this money can be raised through the creation of a Mars One television show.

(Source: Waldron, Ben. "Company Offers One Way Trip to Mars." abcnews.go.com)

nationality of Mars One founder	growing food
part of Mars One training	six billion
number of applicants	one-way
type of trip	over one million
cost of project in dollars	Dutch

MyEnglishLab

Key writing skills and strategies are reinforced and practiced in new contexts. Immediate feedback allows students and teachers to monitor progress and identify areas that need improvement.

x   Welcome to *NorthStar*

Students continue through the writing process to learn revising techniques that help them move toward coherence and unity in their writing. Finally, students edit their work with the aid of a checklist that focuses on essential outcomes.

Los Angeles can (and has) spread out a lot. Although I thought it would be difficult to choose between two dream jobs, it really wasn't because the area near the Ames Research Center is close to my family, has cleaner air, and is less crowded.

1. What choice was the writer faced with?
2. How many reasons did the writer give for the decision?
3. What were the reasons?

2 Complete the outline with information from the paragraph.

I. Topic Sentence: _After graduating, I chose a job at the Ames Research Center in Mountain View (near San Francisco) instead of the job at Jet Propulsion Laboratory in Pasadena (near Los Angeles) for three reasons._

II. Supporting Point: _The first reason was emotional._
   Supporting Details: _I like to attend family get-togethers._
   _____
   _____

III. Supporting Point: _____
   Supporting Details: _____
   _____

IV. Supporting Point: _____
   Supporting Details: _____

3 Look at your answers from Prepare to Write on page 66. Organize your ideas into an outline. Then use your outline to write the first draft of your paragraph. Be sure to include:

- **A topic sentence**
- **Two or three supporting points**. Each one should focus on the reasons for your decision. Then use details to explain each supporting point.
- A co~~~~~~~~~~~~~~~~~~~~~~~

REVISE: Using Parallel Structure

1 Read the sentences about NASA jobs. Label the subjects and the verbs.

- Most people think you have to have an advanced degree to work at NASA, but many jobs do not require engineering or science degrees.
- NASA has locations in California, Texas, Louisiana, Florida, and Maryland.

PARALLEL STRUCTURE

Writers use **parallel structure** when they put two or three words or phrases of the same part of speech (noun, verb, adjective, adverb) together in sentences. The use of parallel structure allows writers to express several ideas in one sentence.

- NASA employees **plan space missions, study weather patterns, fix computers,** and **type letters.**
- NASA is looking for **intelligent, educated,** and **healthy** college graduates to work for them.

Two ideas can be expressed in one sentence:

- When I went online, I **found** the NASA job openings.
- When I went online, I **read** about the types of jobs I could do.
- When I went online, I **found** the NASA job openings and **read** about the types of jobs I could do.

A third idea can be added:

- When I went online, I **applied** for a job.
- When I went online, I **found** the NASA job openings, **read** about the types of jobs I could do, and **applied** for a job.
  *(Notice that **found**, **read**, and **applied** are all in the past tense.)*

Look at two more examples:

    [ADV] [V]   [ADV]   [V]
- I **easily filled** out the application and **successfully submitted** it.
  (The phrases are parallel because they both contain an adverb and a verb.)

               [ADJ]   [N]   [ADJ]   [N]
- I hope the job has a **good environment** and **friendly colleagues.**
  (The phrases are parallel because they both contain an adjective and a noun.)

---

3 Describe your dream job, a job you would like to have. Complete the paragraph. Use parallel structure.

My Dream Job

I would like to work as a / an _____ . This job is _____
                 (name of the job)   (ADJ)
_____, and _____ . People who do this job are talented because
(ADJ)   (ADJ)
they can _____ and _____ . I respect these people because they
        (V)   (V)
work so _____ and _____ . I would like to have this job because of
       (ADV)   (ADV)
its _____ _____ and _____ _____ .
   (ADJ)   (N)   (ADJ)   (N)

4 Now go back to the first draft of your paragraph. Rewrite at least three to four sentences using parallel structure.

━━━━━━━━━━━━━━━━━━━━━━━━━━━━━━━━━ GO TO MyEnglishLab FOR MORE SKILL PRACTICE.

EDIT: Writing the Final Draft

Go to MyEnglishLab and write the final draft of your paragraph. Carefully edit it for grammatical and mechanical errors, such as spelling, capitalization, and punctuation. Make sure you use some of the vocabulary and grammar from the unit. Use the checklist to help you write your final draft. Then submit your paragraph to your teacher.

FINAL DRAFT CHECKLIST

❑ Does your paragraph clearly explain the reasons for your decision?

❑ Does it contain a topic sentence, two or three supporting points, and a concluding sentence?

❑ Does each supporting point focus clearly on one reason?

❑ Are there details to explain each supporting point?

❑ Does the concluding sentence summarize the supporting points (the reasons)?

❑ Are infinitives of purpose used correctly?

❑ Does your paragraph use parallel structure?

❑ Do you use new vocabulary from the unit?

With instant access to a wide range of online content and diagnostic tools, teachers can customize learning environments to meet the needs of every student.

USING MyEnglishLab,
NORTHSTAR TEACHERS CAN:

Deliver rich online content to engage and motivate students, including:

- student audio to support listening and speaking skills.
- engaging, authentic video clips, including reports adapted from ABC, NBC, and CBS newscasts, tied to the unit themes.
- opportunities for written and recorded reactions to be submitted by students.

Use a powerful selection of diagnostic reports to:

- view student scores by unit, skill, and activity.
- monitor student progress on any activity or test as often as needed.
- analyze class data to determine steps for remediation and support.

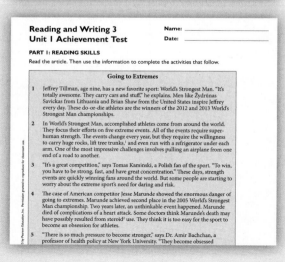

Use Teacher Resource eText* to access:

- a digital copy of the student book for whole class instruction.
- downloadable achievement and placement tests.
- printable resources, including lesson planners, videoscripts, and video activities.
- classroom audio.
- unit teaching notes and answer keys.

---

* Teacher Resource eText is accessible through MyEnglishLab: *NorthStar*.

COMPONENTS   PRINT or eTEXT

STUDENT BOOK and
MyEnglishLab

★ Student Book with MyEnglishLab

The two strands, Reading & Writing and Listening & Speaking, for each of the five levels, provide a fully blended approach with the seamless integration of print and online content. Students use MyEnglishLab to access additional practice online, view videos, listen to audio selections, and receive instant feedback on their work.

eTEXT and
MyEnglishLab

★ eText with MyEnglishLab

Offering maximum flexibility for different learning styles and needs, a digital version of the student book can be used on iPad® and Android® devices.

★ Instructor Access: Teacher Resource eText and MyEnglishLab (Reading & Writing 1–5)

Teacher Resource eText

Each level and strand of *NorthStar* has an accompanying Teacher Resource eText that includes: a digital student book, unit teaching notes, answer keys, downloadable achievement tests, classroom audio, lesson planners, video activities, videoscripts, and a downloadable placement test.

MyEnglishLab

Teachers assign MyEnglishLab activities to reinforce the skills students learn in class and monitor progress through an online gradebook. The automatically-graded exercises in MyEnglishLab *NorthStar* support and build on academic skills and vocabulary presented and practiced in the Student Book/eText. The teacher-graded activities include pronunciation, speaking, and writing, and are assigned by the instructor.

★ Classroom Audio CD

The Listening & Speaking audio contains the recordings and activities as well as audio for the achievement tests. The Reading & Writing strand contains the readings on audio.

SCOPE AND SEQUENCE

UNIT OUTCOMES	1 EXTREME SPORTS SPORTS AND OBSESSION pages 2–23 *Reading 1: An Interview with Travis Binns* *Reading 2: High School Star Hospitalized for Eating Disorder*	2 FRAUD THE CONSEQUENCES OF FRAUD pages 24–47 *Reading 1: Catch Me if You Can: The Frank Abagnale Story* *Reading 2: The Michelle Brown Story: Identity Theft*
READING	• Make and confirm predictions • Identify the main ideas • Identify different types of supporting details • Scan a text to locate specific information • Recognize quotations and reported speech • Organize information using a Venn diagram MyEnglishLab Vocabulary and Reading Skill Practice	• Make and confirm predictions • Identify the main ideas • Identify different types of supporting details • Scan a text to understand chronology • Identify detailed examples MyEnglishLab Vocabulary and Reading Skill Practice
WRITING	• Create an outline answering Wh-questions to gather information • Write a paragraph with a topic sentence, supporting details and a conclusion • Identify the audience and add important details to clarify information • Edit and revise writing for content, language, and conventions **Task:** Write a one-paragraph news report MyEnglishLab Writing Skill Practice and Writing Task	• Organize information by answering questions • Identify correct paragraph structure • Edit and revise writing for content, language, and conventions **Task:** Write a paragraph telling a story MyEnglishLab Writing Skill Practice and Writing Task
INFERENCE	• Infer the writer's degree of certainty	• Infer comparisons
VOCABULARY	• Infer word meaning from context • Recognize and use word forms MyEnglishLab Vocabulary Practice	• Infer word meaning from context • Recognize and understand synonyms • Recognize and use word forms MyEnglishLab Vocabulary Practice
GRAMMAR	• Recognize and use *can, could,* and *be able to* to express ability in the present, past, future, and present perfect MyEnglishLab Grammar Practice	• Distinguish between and use the simple past and past progressive • Recognize and use *when* and *while* MyEnglishLab Grammar Practice
VIDEO	MyEnglishLab *Danny Parks, BMX Pro,* Video Activity	MyEnglishLab *Unhappy Returns,* NBC News, Video Activity
ASSESSMENTS	MyEnglishLab Check What You Know, Checkpoints 1 and 2, Unit 1 Achievement Test	MyEnglishLab Check What You Know, Checkpoints 1 and 2, Unit 2 Achievement Test

3 SPACE
EXPLORING THE RED PLANET
pages 48–73

Reading 1: Mars: Our New Home?
Reading 2: Timeline for a Mission To Mars

4 LANGUAGE
LANGUAGE AND POWER
pages 74–99

Reading 1: Men, Women and Language
Reading 2: The Question of Global English

• Make and confirm predictions • Identify the main ideas • Identify different types of supporting details • Scan a text to locate specific information • Analyze problems and solutions **MyEnglishLab** Vocabulary and Reading Skill Practice	• Make and confirm predictions • Identify the main ideas • Identify different types of supporting details • Scan a text to locate specific information • Recognize opinions and supporting examples **MyEnglishLab** Vocabulary and Reading Skill Practice
• Evaluate pros and cons • Use an outline to organize a paragraph with a main idea, supporting details, and a conclusion • Identify and use parallel structure in academic writing • Edit and revise writing for content, language, and conventions **Task:** Write a paragraph about the pros and cons of building a colony on Mars **MyEnglishLab** Writing Skill Practice and Writing Task	• Organize ideas using a chart • Use an outline to write a paragraph • Recognize and use transitions of contrast • Use transitions of contrast to introduce a counter-argument • Edit and revise writing for content, language, and conventions **Task:** Write a point-by-point contrast paragraph with supporting examples **MyEnglishLab** Writing Skill Practice and Writing Task
• Understand inferred meaning (degrees of difficulty) in a text	• Infer the meanings of proverbs
• Infer word meaning from context • Use knowledge of academic vocabulary to formulate collocations **MyEnglishLab** Vocabulary Practice	• Infer word meaning from context • Recognize and understand antonyms • Recognize and use word forms (nouns, verbs, adjectives, and adverbs) **MyEnglishLab** Vocabulary Practice
• Recognize and express purpose with an infinitive after verbs or after a verb and *in order to* **MyEnglishLab** Grammar Practice	• Recognize and make comparisons with adverbs **MyEnglishLab** Grammar Practice
MyEnglishLab *Life in Space*, ABC News, Video Activity	**MyEnglishLab** *Gender and Communication*, Insight Media, Video Activity
MyEnglishLab Check What You Know, Checkpoints 1 and 2, Unit 3 Achievement Test	**MyEnglishLab** Check What You Know, Checkpoints 1 and 2, Unit 4 Achievement Test

SCOPE AND SEQUENCE

UNIT OUTCOMES	5 CAREERS **CAREERS OF THE FUTURE** pages 100–127 *Reading 1: Meet the New Boss: You* *Reading 2: Great Jobs for the Twenty-first Century*	6 TOURISM **WHAT IS ECOTOURISM?** pages 128–151 *Reading 1: Tourists in a Fragile Land* *Reading 2: A Travel Journal*
READING	• Predict content from a title and subheading in a reading • Identify the main ideas • Recognize details paraphrased from a reading • Scan a text to locate specific information • Categorize information from two texts MyEnglishLab Vocabulary and Reading Skill Practice	• Make and confirm predictions • Identify the main ideas • Identify different types of supporting details • Scan a text to locate specific information • Follow chronological sequence in a reading • Categorize information from two texts MyEnglishLab Vocabulary and Reading Skill Practice
WRITING	• Organize ideas using an outline • Evaluate the structure, format, and content of a cover letter (introduction, supporting points, conclusion) • Edit and revise writing for content, language, and conventions **Task:** Write a cover letter with appropriate content and format MyEnglishLab Writing Skill Practice and Writing Task	• Organize ideas and complete an outline • Identify a thesis statement, topic sentences, and supporting details in a text • Evaluate effective supporting details • Edit and revise writing for content, language, and conventions **Task:** Write an opinion essay with an introduction, body, and conclusion MyEnglishLab Writing Skill Practice and Writing Task
INFERENCE	• Infer author's tone and irony in a reading	• Infer writer's view on probability
VOCABULARY	• Infer word meaning from context • Recognize and use word forms (nouns and adjectives) • Recognize and use synonyms MyEnglishLab Vocabulary Practice	• Infer word meaning from context • Identify relationships between words (synonyms, antonyms, cause/effect, degree) • Use familiar words to form collocations MyEnglishLab Vocabulary Practice
GRAMMAR	• Recognize and use future time clauses and expressions MyEnglishLab Grammar Practice	• Recognize and use *because* and *even though* in main and dependent clauses MyEnglishLab Grammar Practice
VIDEO	MyEnglishLab *Dream Jobs,* ABC News, Video Activity	MyEnglishLab *The Benefits of Ecotourism,* Video Activity
ASSESSMENTS	MyEnglishLab Check What You Know, Checkpoints I and 2, Unit 5 Achievement Test	MyEnglishLab Check What You Know, Checkpoints I and 2, Unit 6 Achievement Test

7 MARRIAGE
FINDING A SPOUSE
pages 152–175

Reading 1: Finding a Spouse
Reading 2: What's Wrong with Tradition?

8 CLIMATE CHANGE
IS OUR CLIMATE CHANGING?
pages 176–204

Reading 1: Our Climate is Changing
Reading 2: Climate Change: Making Informed Decisions

• Make and confirm predictions • Identify the main ideas • Identify different types of supporting details • Scan a text to locate specific information • Recognize and understand metaphors in a reading **MyEnglishLab** Vocabulary and Reading Skill Practice	• Predict content from a title and subheading in a reading • Identify the main ideas • Identify different types of supporting details • Scan a text to locate specific information • Analyze information in a chart • Identify cohesive devises of contrast • Understand and complete a causal chain **MyEnglishLab** Vocabulary and Reading Skill Practice
• Complete a summary • Write a descriptive paragraph • Organize information into logical groups • Use transition words to show degree of importance • Use related word forms to add cohesion to paragraphs • Edit and revise writing for content, language, and conventions **Task:** Write a point-by-point paragraph **MyEnglishLab** Writing Skill Practice and Writing Task	• Summarize cause and effect relationships • Organize ideas using a causal chain • Use cause-and-effect transitions to connect ideas • Write an explanatory paragraph • Edit and revise writing for content, language, and conventions **Task:** Write a cause and effect essay **MyEnglishLab** Writing Skill Practice and Writing Task
• Infer a writer's meaning by comparing two or more pieces of information	• Infer the author's purpose
• Infer word meaning from context • Identify relationships between words (synonyms, antonyms, cause/effect, degree) **MyEnglishLab** Vocabulary Practice	• Infer word meaning from context • Use familiar words to form collocations **MyEnglishLab** Vocabulary Practice
• Distinguish between uses of and use definite/indefinite articles (a/an/the) **MyEnglishLab** Grammar Practice	• Recognize and use *may, might,* and *could* to express future possibility **MyEnglishLab** Grammar Practice
MyEnglishLab *Couples Protect Themselves with Postnup,* ABC News, Video Activity	**MyEnglishLab** *Living the Real Simple Life,* ABC News, Video Activity
MyEnglishLab Check What You Know, Checkpoints 1 and 2, Unit 7 Achievement Test	**MyEnglishLab** Check What You Know, Checkpoints 1 and 2, Unit 8 Achievement Test

ACKNOWLEDGMENTS

Many people helped in the creative process that resulted in this book. We are grateful to Allen Ascher, who first gave us this opportunity, and to everyone at Pearson who contributed to the fourth edition. To Debbie Sistino and Francoise Leffler, who provided clear direction and guidance, many thanks. Most importantly, we want to express my deep appreciation to our editor, Carol Numrich. Her keen insight, understanding of what students need in order to progress, and grace throughout the process will never be forgotten.

—Carolyn Dupaquier
and Laurie Barton

REVIEWERS

Chris Antonellis, Boston University – CELOP; Gail August, Hostos; Aegina Barnes, York College; Kim Bayer, Hunter College; Mine Bellikli, Atilim University; Allison Blechman, Embassy CES; Paul Blomquist, Kaplan; Helena Botros, FLS; James Branchick, FLS; Chris Bruffee, Embassy CES; Nese Cakli, Duzce University; María Cordani Tourinho Dantas, Colégio Rainha De Paz; Jason Davis, ASC English; Lindsay Donigan, Fullerton College; Bina Dugan, BCCC; Sibel Ece Izmir, Atilim University; Érica Ferrer, Universidad del Norte; María Irma Gallegos Peláez, Universidad del Valle de México; Jeff Gano, ASA College; María Genovev a Chávez Bazán, Universidad del Valle de México; Juan Garcia, FLS; Heidi Gramlich, The New England School of English; Phillip Grayson, Kaplan; Rebecca Gross, The New England School of English; Rick Guadiana, FLS; Sebnem Guzel, Tobb University; Esra Hatipoglu, Ufuk University; Brian Henry, FLS; Josephine Horna, BCCC; Arthur Hui, Fullerton College; Zoe Isaacson, Hunter College; Kathy Johnson, Fullerton College; Marcelo Juica, Urban College of Boston; Tom Justice, North Shore Community College; Lisa Karakas, Berkeley College; Eva Kopernacki, Embassy CES; Drew Larimore, Kaplan; Heidi Lieb, BCCC; Patricia Martins, Ibeu; Cecilia Mora Espejo, Universidad del Valle de México; Kate Nyhan, The New England School of English; Julie Oni, FLS; Willard Osman, The New England School of English; Olga Pagieva, ASA College; Manish Patel, FLS; Paige Poole, Universidad del Norte; Claudia Rebello, Ibeu; Lourdes Rey, Universidad del Norte; Michelle Reynolds, FLS International Boston Commons; Mary Ritter, NYU; Minerva Santos, Hostos; Sezer Sarioz, Saint Benoit PLS; Ebru Sinar, Tobb University; Beth Soll, NYU (Columbia); Christopher Stobart, Universidad del Norte; Guliz Uludag, UFUK University; Debra Un, NYU; Hilal Unlusu, Saint Benoit PLS; María del Carmen Viruega Trejo, Universidad del Valle de México; Reda Vural, Atilim University; Douglas Waters, Universidad del Norte; Leyla Yucklik, Duzce University; Jorge Zepeda Porras, Universidad del Valle de México

SPORTS AND Obsession

1 FOCUS ON THE TOPIC

1. Can you name the sport this person is doing? How do you think he feels about his sport?

2. What kind of person participates in this type of sport?

3. How are *extreme sports* different from *non-extreme sports*?

GO TO MyEnglishLab TO CHECK WHAT YOU KNOW.

VOCABULARY

Read the information about rock climbing. Then circle the definition that best matches the meaning of each boldfaced word or phrase.

Some Rock Climbing Facts and History

1. 1800s: People in Europe enjoy climbing the Alps because of the exciting **challenge** of trying to reach the top.

   a. something difficult   **b.** something fun

2. late 1800s: Rock climbing develops as a new sport, separate from mountain climbing. Rock climbers begin to attract public attention with their skill and **daring**.

   a. good looks   **b.** bravery

3. 1887: 17-year-old Georg Winkler **inspires** others with his successful rock climbing before he is killed by mountain snow.

   a. frightens   **b.** motivates

4. 1910s: Some rock climbers are **focused** on developing new equipment that helps people to climb more safely.

   a. giving all your attention to something   **b.** trying to avoid something

5. 1918: Emanuel Frubich completes his **impressive** climb of the Wilder Kopf, considered at the time to be the most difficult climb in the world.

   a. causing admiration   **b.** causing embarrassment

6. 1923: A rating system is developed, using numbers to measure the difficulty and **risk** of climbing a rock.

   a. danger   **b.** excitement

7. 1930s: Rocks with a high rating begin to attract climbers with a **do-or-die** attitude toward the sport.

   a. very foolish   **b.** very determined

8. 1955: With an **obsession** to be the best climber in history, Walter Bonatti spends six days climbing the Dru in the French Alps.

   a. hope of being famous   **b.** very strong interest or desire

9. 1993: Lynn Hill shows **willingness** to climb without equipment as she "free climbs" El Capitan in Yosemite.

   a. being unsure about doing something   **b.** being ready and eager to do something

10. 2007: Chris Sharma becomes known as the world's best rock climber as he completes difficult climbs that are **unthinkable** to the average person.

   a. too scary to do   **b.** too scary to consider

GO TO MyEnglishLab FOR MORE VOCABULARY PRACTICE.

PREVIEW

You are going to read an interview with Travis Binns, the young leader of an international rock climbing club. Before you read, write down three questions that you think the interviewer will ask Travis Binns about his sport and his life.

1. _____

2. _____

3. _____

Now read the interview.

AN INTERVIEW WITH TRAVIS BINNS

1   ***MOUNTAIN HIGH***[1] **(MH):** Let's start with the sport of rock climbing. How did you get interested in this?

2   **TRAVIS BINNS (TB):** It all started when my aunt got married at Joshua Tree National Park. That's in southern California, in the Mojave Desert. She and her groom[2] climbed a rock and exchanged their vows up there. The rest of us stood there, watching them as the sun came up. I was only about five, but I thought it was very cool. That really impressed me.

3   **MH:** Is that what **inspired** you to start rock climbing yourself?

4   **TB:** Yes. But I got even more inspired while watching a video of Alex Honnold doing his solo routine. I saw Alex out there in nature. All by himself, he was able to do the **unthinkable.**

---
[1] ***Mountain High:*** a podcast
[2] **groom:** a man on his wedding day

(continued on next page)

Sports and Obsession   5

5 **MH:** What do you mean by "solo routine"?

6 **TB:** Well, to "free solo" is to go out there without a rope or any gear. It's basically you and your hands and feet. This goes way beyond **daring** into a whole new area of **risk**.

7 **MH:** You climb with your hands and feet? That's it?

8 **TB:** And your incredibly **focused** mind. Alex is a great example of that. People ask him if he does it for the adrenaline rush,[3] and he says no. To him a rush is a sign of something wrong. When the climb's going right, it's slow and controlled. You're enjoying the beautiful day.

9 **MH:** Is Alex Honnold the one who climbed Half Dome in a little under three hours? Without a rope?

10 **TB:** That's the one. He's able to take big chances while staying calm. When he climbs a rock, he's thousands of feet up there, with nothing to catch him if he falls. I guess it takes a real **obsession** to make the most of a talent like his.

11 **MH:** It probably does. Speaking of Half Dome in Yosemite, that's 2,000 feet. Is that one of the places you'll be going with the club?

12 **TB:** Most likely, yes. So far, we've attracted people from six different countries, and they all want to check out Yosemite. It's probably one of the most **impressive** places for doing anything outdoors.

13 **MH:** And you'll be climbing with ropes, the usual gear?

14 **TB:** Of course. We're not part of that tiny group of rock climbers who free solo. I think the number of free solo climbers is less than 1 percent, or something like that. Most of us don't have that **do-or-die** attitude.

15 **MH:** That obsession, you could say.

16 **TB:** And that **willingness** to take a risk. One wrong move and that's it. No second chances. And one of the hardest things about climbing without a rope is staying in control of your fear. You're in a situation where fear can come up in one second—complete and total fear. You've got to stay in control. Alex learned to control his fear in a gym, training 3 hours a day, 6 days a week. He trained hard for the risk of free solo climbing.

17 **MH:** Which brings up an interesting question: is a person selfish to take that kind of risk? Aren't there people who would say to Honnold, "What you're doing is crazy. You'd better quit now while you can."

18 **TB:** I don't know. In Honnold's case, he's a single guy driving around in a van, living a free life. No wife or kids to be responsible for. I think he lives on a thousand dollars a month. He doesn't need much but the rocks and fresh air.

19 **MH:** But he's young enough to have parents, right? What about them?

20 **TB:** I'm sure they've had their moments of worry. But at the same time, I think they probably raised him to value his freedom. I'm sure they taught him to be super-independent. Alex quit a great school, UC Berkeley, so that he could keep climbing up rocks with his bare hands. I think he's done something like one thousand free solo climbs. Crazy!

---

[3] **adrenaline rush:** the body's physical reaction to excitement and danger

21 **MH:** Or obsessed, you might say.

22 **TB:** Yes—and inspirational. People like Alex make us all try harder to push our limits. I heard him say once that he's always pushing himself, and that he's always looking to do something bigger.

23 **MH:** Is that why his friends call him "Alex No Big Deal"?

24 **TB:** Actually, I think that's because he's always saying he's not that great at rock climbing. Maybe he's comparing himself to some idea of the perfect climber, I don't know. Anyways, rock climbing's a great sport, and a lot of us really enjoy the **challenge** of it.

25 **MH:** That's right. Good luck with your club.

26 **TB:** Thanks. You can check the website for more details.

MAIN IDEAS

1 Look again at the Preview on page 5. How did your questions help you understand the interview?

2 Write **T** (true) or **F** (false) for each statement. Rewrite the false statements to make them true.

_____ **1.** Binns became more interested in rock climbing after learning about Alex Honnold.

_____ **2.** A "free solo" climber only uses a rope.

_____ **3.** Free solo climbing is not only a physical challenge but also a mental one.

_____ **4.** Members of the rock climbing club will climb without ropes.

_____ **5.** Alex Honnold had no chance for a university education.

_____ **6.** Other climbers have been inspired by Alex Honnold.

DETAILS

Write one-sentence answers to the questions. Then compare answers with a partner.

1. What impressed Binns as a child?

_____

2. What does Alex Honnold enjoy when a climb is going well?

_____

(continued on next page)

Sports and Obsession   7

3. How high is the northwest face of Half Dome in Yosemite National Park?

_____

4. How many rock climbers complete "free solo" climbs?

_____

5. What is an important part of "free solo" training?

_____

6. Why is Alex Honnold free to focus on rock climbing?

_____

7. How many free solo climbs has Alex Honnold completed?

_____

8. Why does Honnold use the nickname "Alex No Big Deal"?

_____

MAKE INFERENCES

INFERRING CERTAINTY

An **inference** is an **educated guess** about something that is **not directly stated** in a text. A strong reader can **infer how much certainty** is expressed in an interview.

Look at the example and read the explanation.

• "I guess it takes a real obsession to make the most of a talent like his."

How certain is the speaker? Choose the best answer.

a. very certain
b. somewhat certain
(_The best answer is_ **b.**)

When reading an interview, we can infer certainty by looking for **words and phrases** such as _I think, I guess, probably, most likely, maybe,_ or _something like that_. All of these indicate that a speaker is **only somewhat certain** of what he/she says.

When a speaker makes a statement **without these words and phrases**, we infer that he/she is **more certain**.

Sometimes a speaker uses **short statements** to emphasize that he/she is **very certain**.

• "Most of us don't have . . . that willingness to take a risk. <u>One wrong move and that's it.</u> <u>No second chances.</u>"

The two underlined statements are short; from these short statements we can infer that the speaker is very certain of what is being said.

Read each statement. Choose the best answer to indicate how certain the speaker is.

1. I think the number of free solo climbers is less than 1 percent, something like that.

   a. very certain   **b.** not certain

2. You're in a situation where fear can come up in one second—complete and total fear. You've got to stay in control.

   a. very certain   **b.** not certain

3. People like Alex make us all try harder to push our limits.

   a. very certain   **b.** not certain

4. Maybe he's comparing himself to some idea of the perfect climber, I don't know.

   a. very certain   **b.** not certain

5. I'm sure Alex's parents have had their moments of worry.

   a. very certain   **b.** not certain

6. But at the same time, I think they probably raised him to value his freedom.

   a. very certain   **b.** not certain

Now discuss your answers with a partner. Point out the words, phrases, or statements that helped you find the answers.

EXPRESS OPINIONS

Work in groups of three. Choose one of the questions. Discuss your ideas. Then choose one person in your group to report the ideas to the class.

1. What do you think of Alex Honnold's ability to "enjoy the beautiful day" while doing a free solo climb? How would you feel?

2. Do you agree that people who choose to take physical risks are selfish?

3. What do you think of Alex Honnold's decision to drop out of UC Berkeley and focus on rock climbing? Will he regret this decision?

GO TO MyEnglishLab TO GIVE YOUR OPINION ABOUT ANOTHER QUESTION.

READ

1 Look at the boldfaced words and phrases in the reading and think about the questions.

1. Which words or phrases do you know the meanings of?

2. Can you use any of the words or phrases in a sentence?

2 Now read the newspaper article about a high school gymnast.

High School Star Hospitalized for Eating Disorder

1 Vista High School gymnast Ashley Jones was hospitalized Tuesday for **complications** related to anorexia nervosa. Her coach, Dianne Coyle, says that she will not be returning to the gymnastics team this season.

2 "It's really a loss—not only to the team but also to Ashley personally," says Coyle. "She had hopes of qualifying for the Olympics. But her health comes first, of course. Once she is better, I'm sure she can get back into the sport and go for the gold."

3 Dr. Paula Kim, director of the Eating Disorders Clinic at Santa Anita Hospital, explains that it is not unusual for athletes, especially gymnasts, to become obsessed with their weight. One reason for this is that in gymnastics, the lighter the body, the more skillfully it can perform. She explains that an obsession with weight can lead to extreme dieting, which affects not only the body but also the mind.

4 "For the anorexic, the mental focus becomes very small: food and weight. In a way, it's easy to see how this helps the anorexic manage the fear of living in the big, uncontrollable world out there. You may not be able to control how other people feel about you, but you can control what you put in your mouth. You can also control how many hours you spend at the gym. Soon you get hooked on controlling your weight."

5 High school counselor Lisa Rodriguez has expressed concern that Jones's illness is related to pressure.

6 "There's an **enormous** amount of **pressure** that goes along with training for the Olympics," she says. "I know that she comes from a very **accomplished** family—I think that's why she felt she had to achieve so much in sports. Also, when you talk about the Olympics, you're talking about being the best of the best. I think that added to Ashley's feeling of pressure."

7 Since joining the Vista High gymnastics team as a sophomore two years ago, Ashley has broken all school records and led the team to three regional championships.

8 Coach Coyle says, "As soon as I met Ashley, I could tell right away that she was obsessed with the sport. And that's not the kind of athlete that you have to push. My goal with Ashley was to try and help her have more of a balanced life. I talked to her about how she was doing in her classes, what she might want to study in college. I also told her and all the members on the team to take at least one or two days a week just to let their bodies rest. I know it's a very difficult situation, but all I can say is I'm so sorry Ashley got sick."

9 Coyle's concern for Jones's health is shared by her teammates and friends. Some of them

recall how the tiny gymnastics star worked out at the health club in addition to hours of regular practice with the team. They describe how the walls of her bedroom are covered with photos of Olympic winners—Mo Huilan and Gabby Douglas to name a few.

10   Jones, who currently weighs only 72 pounds (32.6 kgs), is expected to remain in the hospital for at least a few months.

COMPREHENSION

Circle the best answer to complete the statements.

1. Ashley's coach hopes that she will leave the hospital and _____.

   a. focus on her health   **b.** join the Olympic team

2. Anorexia nervosa is an obsession with _____.

   a. exercise   **b.** weight

3. One reason for becoming anorexic is that it gives you a feeling of _____.

   a. more control   **b.** mental focus

4. Some of the pressure in Ashley's life was because she wanted to be the best gymnast in _____.

   a. her country   **b.** the world

5. Before she went to the hospital, her coach had been pushing her to focus on gymnastics _____.

   a. less   **b.** more

GO TO MyEnglishLab FOR MORE VOCABULARY PRACTICE.

READING SKILL

1 **Read a statement from Reading Two again. Then answer the questions.**

> "Ashley had hopes of qualifying for the Olympics. But her health comes first, of course. Once she is better, I'm sure she can get back into the sport and go for the gold."

Who is speaking here? Is it Ashley or someone else? How do we know?

RECOGNIZING QUOTATIONS AND REPORTED SPEECH

In a **news article**, both **quotations and reported speech** are used:

A **quotation** includes **quotation marks** to indicate that a person's **exact words** are being reported.

- "It's really a loss—not only to the team but also to Ashley personally," says Coyle.

Reported speech does not include quotation marks and is an **explanation** of what someone has said. In reported speech, **different words** may be used to express the original meaning.

- Her coach, Dianne Coyle, says that she will not be returning to the gymnastics team this season.

Most **news articles** include the names of several people. As you read news articles, it is important to **pay attention to names** of people and also to **pronouns** that refer to these people. This will help you to **keep track of what people** in the article **have done and said**. As a result, you will understand the article more clearly.

2 **Work with a partner to answer the questions about Reading Two.**

1. Read **paragraph 2**. Is this a quotation or reported speech?

2. Who is speaking in **paragraph 3**?

3. Read **paragraph 5**. Is this a quotation or reported speech?

4. Who is speaking in **paragraph 6**?

5. Read **paragraph 8**. Is this a quotation or reported speech?

6. In the same paragraph, who is being referred to by the pronouns *her* and *their*?

GO TO MyEnglishLab *FOR MORE SKILL PRACTICE.*

STEP 1: Organize

Look at the list of characteristics and at the Venn diagram. Put characteristics that describe Alex Honnold in the left circle, characteristics that describe Ashley Jones in the right circle, and those that describe both athletes in the middle part where the two circles overlap.

Characteristics

- competitive
- enjoyment of sport
- strongly focused
- need to feel in control
- fearless
- world seems beautiful

- world seems scary
- family is supportive
- family adds pressure
- obsession leads to success
- obsession leads to illness
- obsession related to being perfect

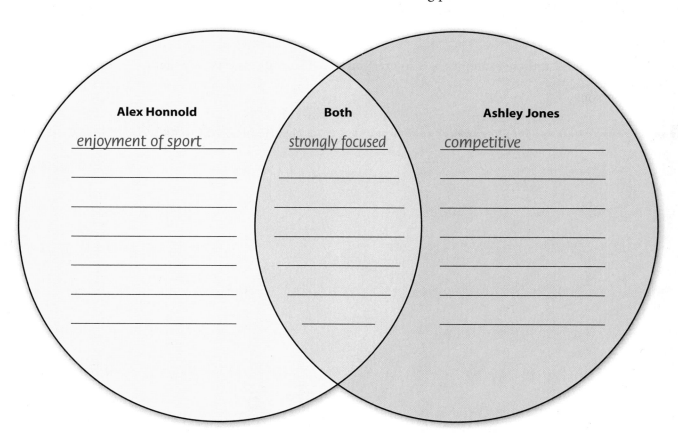

Alex Honnold

enjoyment of sport

_____

_____

_____

_____

_____

Both

strongly focused

_____

_____

_____

_____

_____

Ashley Jones

competitive

_____

_____

_____

_____

_____

Work with a partner. Complete the short essay about obsession with what you know about Alex Honnold and Ashley Jones. Use your Venn diagram from Step 1.

Obsession can be helpful or destructive, depending on the person. This can be clearly seen in two examples from the sports world. Alex Honnold and Ashley Jones are both

_____ *strongly focused* _____

_____ .

In addition, _____ .

However, there are important differences between them. Alex Honnold _____

_____ .

Ashley Jones _____ .

Also, _____ .

As we look at these examples, it is interesting to see how obsession can either help or harm a person.

■■ *GO TO* MyEnglishLab *TO CHECK WHAT YOU LEARNED.*

VOCABULARY

REVIEW

Read the paragraph about the Academy Award-winning actress Natalie Portman. Complete the paragraph with the words from the box. Not all the words will be used.

accomplished	daring	focused	~~obsession~~	unthinkable
challenge	do-or-die	impressive	pressure	willingness
complications	enormous	inspire	risk	

An Amazing Performance

In 2011 Natalie Portman won an Academy Award for her role in *Black Swan*, a film about a ballerina who develops an _____obsession_____ with performing a
1.
role. To prepare for the film, Portman made an _____ effort to exercise
2.
each day for six months, practicing ballet and increasing her fitness. As a result of her _____ to work very hard to train
3.
her body, Portman gave a convincing performance as Nina, a ballerina who faces several

_____ of mental illness that lead her to _____ fantasies in a
4.   5.
_____ to take her art to a higher level. As Nina faces the _____
6.   7.
of having to compete with another dancer, she takes a _____ approach to being
8.
the best. She is so _____ on her role that she faces the _____
9.   10.
of losing her mind as she pushes herself to go beyond her limits and shows her strength and

_____. Portman's amazing performance in this film will _____
11.   12.
other actresses for years to come.

Complete the chart with the correct word forms. Some categories can have more than one form. Use a dictionary if necessary. An **X** indicates that you do not need to put a form in that category.

	NOUN	VERB	ADJECTIVE	ADVERB
1.	*accomplishment*		accomplished	X
2.	challenge			X
3.	complication			X
4.	a. daring b.			
5.		X	enormous	
6.			focused	X
7.			impressive	
8.		inspire		
9.	obsession		a. b. obsessive	
10.	pressure			X
11.	risk			X
12.	willingness	X		

CREATE

Write a paragraph describing one of your achievements, hobbies, or goals. Use at least five of the words from the box in your paragraph. You may change the form of the word.

accomplished	daring	focused	obsession	unthinkable
challenge	do-or-die	impressive	pressure	willingness
complications	enormous	inspire	risk	

GO TO MyEnglishLab FOR MORE VOCABULARY PRACTICE.

GRAMMAR

1 Look at the following examples from Reading Two. Think about the meaning of the boldfaced words.

- As soon as I met Ashley, I **could** tell right away that she was obsessed with the sport.

- You may not **be able to** control how other people feel about you, but you **can** control what you put in your mouth.

- You **can** also control how many calories you put in your mouth.

ABILITY: *CAN, BE ABLE TO, COULD*

1. *Can* describes ability in the present.	He **can** climb Half Dome in Yosemite.
2. *Be able to* describes ability in the present.	She **is able to** swim fast. *(present)* He**'s not able to** ride a horse. *(negative present)*
3. *Could* or *was / were able to* describes general ability in the past.	When he was a boy, he **could** ride his bike all day. Last winter, they **were able to** ski four times. He **wasn't able to** join the Olympic team. *(negative past)*
4. Use *be able to* to describe ability in forms other than present tense (*can*) or past tense (*could*).	They **will be able to** win the race. *(future)* They **have been able to** win two championships. *(present perfect)*

2 A young rock climber wrote a letter to Alex Honnold. Complete the sentences with **can, can't, could, couldn't,** or **be able to** to express ability.

Dear Mr. Honnold,

My name is Dylan Gonzalez, and I live in San Diego, CA. I am 15 years old, and I'm obsessed with rock climbing. It's all I _____ think about! My dream is to _____
    1.   2.
free solo climb like you do. I really _____ believe your willingness to take a risk!
                        3.
Last week I went camping and tried to climb some rocks, but I _____ get very far.
                                    4.
My mom came over and started yelling at me. She didn't think I _____ do it safely
                                    5.
enough, but I told her not to worry.

I'm a pretty good rock climber for my age. How old were you when you _____
                                    6.
finally do a free solo climb? I want to _____ do that by my eighteenth birthday.
                7.
I'm going to practice a lot.

Mr. Honnold, I know that you're really busy with all your climbs, but I really hope that you
will _____ write me back very soon. Maybe you _____ find time
    8.   9.
for a rock climbing star of the future.

Thanks for reading my letter. Keep up the impressive rock climbing. You're the best!

Yours truly,

Dylan Gonzalez

3 On a separate piece of paper, write down five statements about yourself, each using a different verb expressing ability from the list in the box. Write some statements that are true and some statements that are false. Exchange papers with a classmate. Guess which statements are true and which are false.

be able to	not be able to	can	can't	could	couldn't

■■■■■■■■■■■■■■■■■■■ *GO TO* MyEnglishLab *FOR MORE GRAMMAR PRACTICE AND TO CHECK WHAT YOU LEARNED.*

FINAL WRITING TASK

In this unit, you read about Alex Honnold, a rock climber who is famous for his free solo climbs. Now imagine that you are a newspaper reporter. You are going to *write a factual report (one paragraph) about Alex Honnold's completion of the Triple, an amazing rock climbing achievement*. Use the vocabulary and grammar from the unit.*

PREPARE TO WRITE: Group Brainstorming

1 Work in a small group. On a piece of paper, brainstorm questions you would want to ask Alex Honnold about his free solo climb up Half Dome in Yosemite. Think of as many questions as you can and write them down. Do not worry about spelling and grammar.

2 Share your list with the class. The teacher will write the questions on the board.

WRITE: A Factual Report

1 Look back at the newspaper article in Reading Two. How is it different from the style of Reading One? What do you think is the purpose of the newspaper article?

USING THE 5WS TO WRITE A FACTUAL REPORT

A news article is an example of a **factual report**. Good newspaper articles **answer five basic questions**—called the **5Ws**. Important information includes:

- **Who** is the story about?
- **What** is the story about?
- **When** did the story take place?
- **Where** did the story take place?
- **Why** or **How** did the story happen?

In a factual report, **quotations** (people's exact words) may also be used to give more facts or opinions.

---

* For Alternative Writing Topics, see page 23. These topics can be used in place of the writing topic for this unit or as homework. The alternative topics relate to the theme of the unit but may not target the same grammar or rhetorical structures taught in the unit.

2 Go back to the interview in Reading One. Think like a newspaper reporter. Write five questions you would want to ask Alex Honnold about completing the Triple, using the **5Ws**.

1. Who _____

2. What _____

3. When _____

4. Where _____

5. Why/How _____

3 Look at the facts about Honnold's climb. Match them with the correct categories. Write the correct letter in the blank before each fact. You may write a letter more than once.

> **Categories**
> **a.** Who completed the Triple?
> **b.** What is the Triple?
> **c.** When did Alex Honnold complete the Triple?
> **d.** Where did he do it?
> **e.** How long did the climb take?
> **f.** Why is this climb so impressive?

Facts

_a_ **1.** Alex Honnold made history when he completed the Triple.

_____ **2.** Climbing the Triple includes climbing three very large rock surfaces in Yosemite Park: Mount Watkins, El Capitan, and Half Dome.

_____ **3.** Only a small number of climbers in the world can complete this 7,000-foot climb in 24 hours.

_____ **4.** The Triple is located in one of Honnold's favorite climbing spots, Yosemite National Park in California.

_____ **5.** On Mount Watkins, Honnold kept his balance even while climbing through insects that covered his ears, neck, and mouth.

_____ **6.** As he completed the Triple in June 2012, crowds of people waited to congratulate him.

(continued on next page)

_____ **7.** During most of the climb, Honnold used no rope at all.

_____ **8.** Honnold completed the Triple in record time: 18 hours and 50 minutes.

_____ **9.** It would only take one mistake for Honnold to fall and die.

_____ **10.** Honnold was the first climber to complete the Triple alone.

4 Plan the first draft of your paragraph by completing the outline. Use the **5Ws** information to explain how Alex Honnold completed the Triple.

    1. Write a **topic sentence** that states the main idea of your paragraph.

    _____

    _____

    2. Give at least **five supporting details** (based on the 5Ws).

    _____

    _____

    _____

    _____

    _____

    3. Write a **concluding sentence** which restates the main idea of the topic sentence in a new way.

    _____

    _____

5 Use your outline and your notes from Prepare to Write, page 18, and Step 1, page 13, to write the first draft of your paragraph.

ADDING MORE INFORMATION FOR GREATER CLARITY

When you write, think about your **audience**, the people who will read what you write. Remember that they may know less about the topic than you do. Make sure you **clearly explain new words or expressions**.

- **Sentence:** Vista High School gymnast Ashley Jones was hospitalized Tuesday for complications related to anorexia nervosa.
- **Problem:** Some people may not know what anorexia nervosa is.
- **Revised sentence:** Vista High School gymnast Ashley Jones was hospitalized Tuesday for complications related to anorexia nervosa, *an illness in which the person is obsessed with dieting*.

There are several **ways to add more information to a sentence**:

1. Add more information, between commas, **in the middle** of the sentence.

   - Dr. Paula Kim, *director of the Eating Disorders Clinic at Baldwin Hospital*, explains that it is not unusual for athletes to become obsessed with their weight.

2. Add more information after a comma **at the end** of the sentence.

   - She explains that an obsession with weight can lead to extreme dieting, *which affects not only the body but also the mind*.

1 Read the paragraph. The underlined words need more explanation. Use the explanations that follow to rewrite the sentences on a separate piece of paper. Compare your answers with a classmate's.

According to ANRED, eating disorders continue to be on the rise among athletes, especially in sports that emphasize being thin. Sports such as gymnastics, figure skating, dancing, and synchronized swimming have a higher percentage of athletes with eating disorders. According to an American College of Sports Medicine study, eating disorders affected 62% of the females in these sports. Christy Henrich died of anorexia in 1994. Anorexia nervosa affects about one percent of female adolescents in the United States. Bulimia nervosa affects about four percent of college-aged women. If you want more information, contact the NEDIC.

a. ANRED = Anorexia Nervosa and Related Eating Disorders, an organization that provides information about eating disorders

b. Christy Henrich = a top United States gymnast in the late 1980s

(continued on next page)

Sports and Obsession 21

c. anorexia nervosa = an eating disorder in which the person diets so much that they become too thin

d. bulimia nervosa = an eating disorder in which the person diets, becomes hungry, overeats, and then vomits to get rid of the food

e. NEDIC = National Eating Disorder Information Center

2 Now go back to the first draft of your paragraph. Are there any words or expressions that another reader may not understand? Underline anything that needs to be explained, find out the explanations, and add them where needed in your paragraph. Make sure you use the correct punctuation.

■■■ *GO TO* MyEnglishLab *FOR MORE SKILL PRACTICE.*

EDIT: Writing the Final Draft

Go to My EnglishLab and write the final draft of your paragraph. Carefully edit it for grammatical and mechanical errors, such as spelling, capitalization, and punctuation. Make sure you use some of the vocabulary and grammar from the unit. Use the checklist to help you write your final draft. Then submit your paragraph to your teacher.

FINAL DRAFT CHECKLIST

❏ Does your topic sentence state the main idea of the paragraph?

❏ Does your paragraph answer the 5Ws?

❏ Are the supporting details in order?

❏ Do you use quotations to give more facts or opinions?

❏ Does the concluding sentence restate the main idea of the topic sentence in a new way?

❏ Did you add information to explain words or expressions that were unclear?

❏ Do you use *can, could,* or *be able to* to express ability?

❏ Do you use new vocabulary from the unit?

UNIT PROJECT

Choose an athlete or dancer famous in your community. Write a factual report (one paragraph) about his or her life and accomplishments. Follow these steps:

STEP 1: Find a person in your community who has had significant accomplishments in sports or dance. Interview the person.
You may also gather information about the person by reading local newspaper articles and/or searching the Internet.

STEP 2: Use the information to write a factual report about this person's life and accomplishments. Refer to the following questions in writing your report.

- **Who** is this person? What kind of early life and education did he or she have? Who are other important people related to this person?

- **What** are the greatest accomplishments of this person? What kind of problems did he or she have to face?

- **When** did this person become well-known? When and where did this person's accomplishments take place?

- **Where** did this person first become involved in sports or dance? Where has this person traveled?

- **Why** has this person become so successful? How much training and practice has been involved? Has obsession helped them in any way?

STEP 3: Read your report to a small group of classmates.

ALTERNATIVE WRITING TOPICS

Write about one of the topics. Use the vocabulary and grammar from the unit.

1. Write a factual report (one paragraph) about a famous athlete that you admire. Why do you admire him or her? What has this athlete accomplished?

2. There are other activities that can lead to a dangerous obsession. Some people enjoy watching their favorite movie stars so much that they begin stalking, or obsessively following, the stars. Other examples include shopping and using the Internet. Write a report (one paragraph) explaining how obsession with an activity can become dangerous. Give some examples about obsessions of people you know or people in the news.

■■■■■■■■■■■■■■■ GO TO MyEnglishLab TO PRACTICE INTERNET SKILLS, WRITE ABOUT ONE OF THE ALTERNATIVE TOPICS, WATCH A VIDEO ABOUT A PROFESSIONAL BMX BIKER, AND TAKE THE UNIT 1 ACHIEVEMENT TEST. ■■■

THE CONSEQUENCES OF
Fraud

1 FOCUS ON THE TOPIC

1. There are many types of fraud, for example, medical fraud, Internet fraud, and identity theft.[1] What type of fraud does the photo illustrate?

2. What are some other kinds of fraud?

3. Is fraud more or less common today than in the past? Why or why not?

---

[1] **identity theft:** a type of fraud in which a person's banking and other information is used by a criminal, usually to buy things

GO TO MyEnglishLab *TO CHECK WHAT YOU KNOW.*

VOCABULARY

1 Read the online article about fraud. Pay attention to the boldfaced words.

TYPES OF FRAUD

Fraud has been increasing around the world because of computer technology. One example is the Nigerian Bank Fraud. People are contacted by email and asked to help transfer money from Nigeria or other African countries by allowing the money to be placed temporarily in their bank accounts. The real **motive** is not to transfer money but to obtain personal banking information.

Another type of computer fraud is known as "phishing," or trying to obtain financial information by **impersonating** a bank employee. When this kind of fraud takes place, you receive email messages from someone pretending to represent your bank. You are then asked to provide your account number or other identifying information. This kind of **deception** seems so real that many people respond to it and give away their financial and personal information.

The telephone is also used by **con men and women** who try to impress people with amazing prizes and offers. Sometimes they will call and ask for your banking information so that they can put prize money into your account. If you do not trust a person contacting you by phone, ask for his or her name, business phone number, and company address. You can then contact the company yourself to learn whether or not you have reason to be **suspicious**.

Modern communications technology has made it easier for people to trick you with **fake** deals and requests for information. When you go online, you find many websites offering products and services such as medical treatment and legal advice. How can you know if something is real? Fortunately, there are many organizations that can help you make sure that companies and individuals are treating you with **honesty**. If you believe that you are involved in a case of fraud, be sure to report it and ask for help.

2 Circle the correct synonym for each boldfaced word.

1. A **fraud** is a trick to get _____.

   a. money or power   **b.** computers

2. A person's **motive** for doing something is his or her _____.

   a. reason   **b.** reward

3. If you **impersonate** a bank employee, you _____.

   a. really are one   **b.** are pretending to be one

4. When **deception** takes place, people _____.

   a. tell the truth   **b.** lie

5. A **con man or woman** is someone who is trying to _____.

   a. trick you   **b.** help you

6. When you are **suspicious** of someone, you _____.

   a. believe them   **b.** don't believe them

7. A **fake** deal is one that is _____.

   a. real   **b.** not real

8. When people treat you with **honesty**, they are telling you _____.

   a. the truth   **b.** lies

--- GO TO MyEnglishLab *FOR MORE VOCABULARY PRACTICE.*

PREVIEW

You are going to read the true story of Frank Abagnale, a former con man. Before you read, look at the list below. Check (✓) three types of fraud that you think you might read about in the story.

_____ **1.** impersonation   _____ **4.** Internet fraud

_____ **2.** telephone fraud   _____ **5.** document fraud

_____ **3.** selling fake products   _____ **6.** bank fraud

Now read Frank Abagnale's story.

Catch Me If You Can: The Frank Abagnale Story

1 A doctor . . . a lawyer . . . an airline pilot . . . a college professor . . . former **con man** Frank Abagnale played all these roles as a young man, stealing millions of dollars from banks around the world. His money-making secret? Cashing false checks. His **motive** for playing different roles? Respect and excitement. He enjoyed having other people believe that he was important.

2 He first **impersonated** an airline pilot by wearing a pilot's uniform. Then he created a phony airline ID. The result was very exciting to him. Abagnale never operated a plane, but he used his pilot uniform to fly for free and to date attractive young flight attendants. Then he discovered a luxury apartment community[1] near Atlanta, Georgia. He paid cash for six months' rent in advance and wrote "medical doctor" on his apartment application. He soon became friends with a doctor in the apartment community. After convincing this man that he, too, was a medical doctor, he was offered a hospital job as a temporary supervisor.

Abagnale performed this role by relying on nurses and medical students to do all the work while he simply pretended to be in charge. But finally, when faced with a life-or-death situation involving a newborn baby, Abagnale decided that he could no longer continue the **deception**. He knew that if he kept impersonating a doctor, an innocent child might die. Still, before leaving his hospital job, Abagnale made sure to get his paycheck.

3 Next, he dated another flight attendant, whom he impressed by claiming that he had graduated from law school. She introduced him to a real lawyer, who immediately offered him a position as a state attorney. Abagnale accepted the offer, but he needed to create a **fake** transcript from Harvard Law School. He also needed to pass the state law exam. He studied for several weeks but failed the eight-hour exam on his first and second attempts. When he tried a third time, he passed and became a licensed attorney despite the fact that he had never finished high school. He worked as a lawyer for nine months before he met a genuine Harvard graduate who started asking him specific questions about the school and its professors. Because Abagnale could not answer these questions, the man became **suspicious** and started questioning Abagnale's **honesty**.

4 The young con man escaped from this uncomfortable situation by heading to the western United States. There he visited college campuses in Utah, where he was impressed

---

[1] **luxury apartment community:** an area with very expensive and comfortable apartments

with the beauty of female students. He decided to apply for a summer teaching position, which he obtained by making a fake transcript from Columbia University and writing false letters of recommendation. Abagnale was quite happy to work as a "professor." To prepare for class, he simply used the textbook, making sure to stay one chapter ahead of the students. Abagnale also discussed his own personal experiences in class, and the students responded with much interest. But when summer school ended, he could no longer stay in Utah. He knew that the FBI was searching for him because he had been cashing phony checks all over the country. He moved to California and eventually to France, thinking he could live quietly and safely there. However, he was wrong.

5   In France, Abagnale was recognized by a flight attendant and reported to the authorities. Soon, he was in a French prison, where he almost died because of very little food and very dirty surroundings. After six months, he was sent to a prison in Sweden. He learned that police in several European countries were waiting to arrest him for check **fraud**, and he feared that prison conditions in other places might be even worse than those in France. Eventually, Sweden sent him to the United States, where he spent four years in federal prison.

6   After his release, Abagnale had a problem shared by many other criminals: limited job opportunities. He worked hard in various entry-level positions and showed the ability to become a top manager but could not get any high positions because of his prison background. He thought about returning to a life of crime but decided instead to offer his services as a "white-collar crime specialist" teaching banks and other businesses how to avoid becoming the victims of fraud. Soon he was offered a position working with the FBI Financial Crimes Unit. Today, he runs his own company. It specializes in protecting checks and other documents against fraud.

7   His first book, *Catch Me If You Can*, was made into a Steven Spielberg film in 2002. In one interview, he was asked if he had ever thought about becoming an actor, considering his skill at impersonation. The answer was no. The real Frank Abagnale is satisfied with his real life as a company owner and family man.

MAIN IDEAS

1 Look again at the Preview on page 27. How did your predictions help you understand the story?

2 Put the events of Frank Abagnale's life in chronological order.

_____ **a.** He finally succeeds in passing his law exam.

_____ **b.** He moves from France to Sweden.

_____ **c.** He starts his own company.

__1__ **d.** He impersonates an airline pilot.

_____ **e.** He quits his hospital job.

_____ **f.** He decides to teach a college class.

DETAILS

Choose the letter of the best ending on the right to complete each sentence on the left.

1. Abagnale used his uniform to gain __j__ .

2. He got his hospital job with the help of _____.

3. He quit impersonating a doctor after dealing with _____.

4. He passed his law exam after _____.

5. He was hired as a college professor because of _____.

6. In the United States and Europe, he made money by cheating _____.

7. He was afraid of _____.

8. When he left prison, he was unable to get _____.

9. Today he is employed as _____.

10. He thought about continuing his career as _____.

11. Despite his talents, he is not interested in _____.

a. banks

b. high-level jobs

c. fake recommendations

d. a crime expert

e. a sick baby

f. acting

g. bad prison conditions

h. a criminal

i. several attempts

j. free travel

k. a neighbor

MAKE INFERENCES

INFERRING COMPARISONS

An **inference** is an **educated guess** about something that is **not directly stated** in a text. Writers sometimes suggest comparisons without directly stating them. A strong reader can **infer** these **comparisons** by reading the text closely.

Look at the example and read the explanation.

• Frank Abagnale was more successful _____.

Choose the best way to complete the comparison statement.

a. cashing false checks

b. deceiving people in the medical world
   (*The best answer is* **b.**)

In **paragraph 2** we learn that Abagnale worked in a hospital but made <u>his own</u> decision to leave the hospital because an innocent child might die. He worked in a hospital but he chose to leave. (*He was successful.*)

In **paragraph 4** we learn that the FBI was searching for him because he had been cashing phony checks. *(He was not successful.)*

In **paragraph 5** we learn that several European countries were waiting to arrest him for check fraud. *(He was not successful.)*

After reading the text closely, we **can infer** that Abagnale was more successful deceiving people in the medical world than he was at cashing false checks.

Choose the best way to complete each comparison statement. Refer to the paragraphs in parentheses.

1. Frank Abagnale had an easier time impressing _____. *(paragraphs 2 and 3)*

   a. flight attendants   **b.** lawyers

2. Frank Abagnale was more successful at getting a job as a _____. *(paragraphs 3 and 4)*

   a. lawyer   **b.** professor

3. Prison conditions were better for Frank Abagnale in _____. *(paragraph 5)*

   a. France   **b.** the United States

Now discuss your answers with a partner. Point out the sentences in the paragraphs that helped you find the answers.

EXPRESS OPINIONS

Work in groups of three. Choose one of the questions. Discuss your ideas. Then choose one person in your group to report the ideas to the class.

1. Which of Abagnale's impersonations do you think was the most dangerous? Why?

2. What do you think was more important to Abagnale—money or respect?

3. Do you think that Abagnale was punished fairly for his fraud? Explain your answer.

■■■■■■■■■■■■■■■■■■■■■■■■■■■■■■ *GO TO MyEnglishLab TO GIVE YOUR OPINION ABOUT ANOTHER QUESTION.*

READ

1 Look at the boldfaced words and phrases in the reading and think about the questions.

1. Which words or phrases do you know the meanings of?

2. Can you use any of the words or phrases in a sentence?

2 Now read the story of Michelle Brown, a real woman who experienced identity theft. The story appears in *The Art of the Steal* by Frank Abagnale.

THE MICHELLE BROWN STORY: IDENTITY THEFT

1   It began on a winter day with a seemingly ordinary message on an answering machine. It was from someone at the bank. Something about her new Dodge Ram pickup and the payment past due on the loan . . .

2   Michelle Brown was a single woman in her late twenties. She lived in southern California and worked as a credit analyst.[1] She was cheerful, and people found her fun to be around. Friends were always telling her how she was too nice. She worked hard and was tidy with her finances. She owned 15 credit cards but had never been late on a single payment. Ever since she was 17, she had perfect credit. She liked everything in her life to be perfect.

3   She returned the call. She told the bank officer that there had to be a mistake; she hadn't bought a truck. The officer quickly agreed that he must have the wrong Michelle Brown. The phone numbers on the credit application weren't working . . . To prove beyond a doubt that it was another Michelle Brown he was searching for, she told him her Social Security number. She was stunned—it was the same one that was on the application.

4   Alarmed, she called up the credit reporting agencies[2] and told them that something **fishy** was going on. They put a fraud alert on her credit and promised to send out a report on her recent purchases. She checked with the Division of Motor Vehicles and learned something **astonishing**: a **duplicate** driver's license had recently been issued to a Michelle Brown. Someone else was using her name, her address, her Social Security number, and her driver's license. It was as if someone was slowly erasing her identity . . .

5   When her credit report arrived, there were delinquent[3] bills on it for thousands of dollars, including a sizable phone bill and even a bill for liposuction treatments.[4] What was this? She became afraid to open her own

---

[1] **credit analyst:** a bank employee who studies customers' bill-paying records
[2] **credit reporting agencies:** organizations that keep track of bill-paying records
[3] **delinquent:** late in paying money that is owed
[4] **liposuction treatments:** a type of cosmetic surgery in which body fat is removed

mailbox, for fear of what new debt would be awaiting her. In time, she would learn that there was an arrest warrant[5] out for Michelle Brown in Texas. The charge was conspiracy[6] to sell marijuana. She had never broken a law, any law. How could she be wanted by the police?

6   She began to worry that the other Michelle Brown would break into her apartment in search of her passport or checks, or who knew what else. Whenever she got home after dark she carried a flashlight and searched through the rooms, including every closet. She was **weary** and angry. When she went to bed at night, she was scared. If she heard the slightest noise, her first thought was that the woman calling herself Michelle Brown was out there in the dark, right beneath her window. Who was this person who was stealing her identity? Why of all the people in the world, did she pick her? And what did she want?

---

[5] **arrest warrant:** a document giving police the authority to take someone to jail
[6] **conspiracy:** a secret plan by two or more people to do something illegal

COMPREHENSION

Read the statements and mark them **T** (true) or **F** (false). Rewrite the false statements to make them true.

_____ **1.** Michelle Brown was careless with her finances.

_____ **2.** One form of identification was stolen from her.

_____ **3.** The person who stole her identity made a variety of purchases.

_____ **4.** She began selling drugs as a way of paying her bills.

_____ **5.** Identity theft affected her emotionally as well as financially.

GO TO MyEnglishLab *FOR MORE VOCABULARY PRACTICE.*

READING SKILL

1 Read paragraph 2 of Reading Two again. How do we know Michelle was tidy with her finances? Underline the sentences, phrases, and words that give information about how Michelle was tidy with her finances.

IDENTIFYING DETAILED EXAMPLES

To understand the main ideas of a text, readers need to **identify** and understand the **detailed examples** that **support and explain** these **ideas**.

Detailed examples include information about **time, place, people** and **events**.

Main Idea | Detailed Examples

- Michelle Brown liked her life to be perfect. She worked hard and was tidy with her finances. She had never been late on a single credit card payment. Ever since she was 17 she had perfect credit.

Signal words such as *for example, for instance, such as, including, in addition,* and *in fact* sometimes explain the connection between the ideas and the detailed examples.

Main Idea | Detailed Examples

- Michelle Brown liked her life to be perfect. *For example*, Michelle worked hard and was tidy with her finances. *In addition*, she had never been late on a single credit card payment. *In fact*, ever since she was 17 she had perfect credit.

The first sentence expresses the main idea. The following sentences give detailed examples to support and explain that idea.

2 Work with a partner. Read paragraphs 4 and 5 of Reading Two again. Answer the questions.

1. **Paragraph 4:** What examples are given to explain Michelle's identity theft?

2. **Paragraph 5:** What examples of delinquent bills are mentioned?

GO TO MyEnglishLab *FOR MORE SKILL PRACTICE.*

STEP 1: Organize

Reading One (**R1**) and Reading Two (**R2**) contain information about the financial consequences of fraud. Look at the list of consequences below. Place them in the appropriate category by writing the letter of each consequence in the chart.

FINANCIAL CONSEQUENCES OF FRAUD	
IMPERSONATION (R1)	IDENTITY THEFT (R2)
_a_	___
___	___
___	___

a. Banks lost money as many fake checks were cashed.

b. Brown faced delinquent bills and new debt.

c. Someone had bought a new truck with Brown's credit.

d. Legal clients paid for the services of a false lawyer.

e. A hospital lost money paying Abagnale's paycheck.

f. A fraud alert was placed on Brown's credit.

STEP 2: Synthesize

Imagine that Frank Abagnale is interviewing Michelle Brown for his book *The Art of the Steal*. Work with a partner to complete their conversation with information from the chart in Step 1. Add detailed examples to support their ideas.

FRANK: Fraud can often have financial consequences on more than one individual. I know that when I impersonated people, _____

_____

_____

What were the financial consequences when your identity was stolen?

MICHELLE: Well, there were several. _____

_____

_____

GO TO MyEnglishLab TO CHECK WHAT YOU LEARNED.

3 FOCUS ON WRITING

VOCABULARY

REVIEW

Read the article about a man who was practicing medicine without a license. Complete the article with the words from the box. One word is not used.

astonishing	duplicate	~~fraud~~	motive
con man	fake	honesty	suspicious
deception	fishy	impersonate	weary

PHONY[1] DOCTOR GETS 12 YEARS IN PRISON

John E. Curran will spend 12 years in prison because he pretended to be a doctor. In this case

of medical _____fraud_____, he lied to sick people and said that he could cure them with
    1.

his "natural" medicine. To _____ a doctor, Curran bought _____
                                    2.   3.

medical degrees on the Internet for $2,650. It was even more _____ that he
                                                                      4.

received a "medical degree" from the Asian American Institute in Costa Rica in only two months.

This made him seem like a real doctor. He wore a lab coat with MD[2] after his name and checked

people's blood. He told them they had cancer or other illnesses. Then he sold them "E-Water" and

"Green Drink"—two products that would cure them, he said. He also charged people $10,000

for the use of medical machines that he kept in his office. Curran impressed people with his false

medical knowledge. They were _____ of feeling sick and believed his "natural"
                                        5.

medicine could help them. One woman, however, became _____ of Curran after
                                                                6.

paying $1,200 a month for his "Green Drink." After three months, Curran refused to check her

blood, and she thought this was _____. She went to another doctor and learned
                                        7.

that Curran's medicine was not real: it was all a _____. In court, Curran asked the
                                                            8.

_____

[1] **phony:** fake or false
[2] **MD:** medical doctor

judge not to give him a strong punishment. He claimed that he was acting with complete

_____ and that he really wanted to help people with his medicine. He asked the
          9.

judge to be kind to him. But the judge responded that Curran's _____ was not
                                                                              10.

helping people but wanting to make money. Because the judge believed that money was the

reason for Curran's actions, he gave him 12 years in prison. "You are the worst of the worst," said

the judge, believing Curran to be a liar, a _____.
                                                    11.

EXPAND

1 Complete the chart with the correct word forms. Some categories can have more than one form. Use a dictionary if necessary. An **X** indicates that you do not need to write a form in that category.

	NOUN	VERB	ADJECTIVE	ADVERB
1.	deception	*deceive*		
2.			duplicate	X
3.	a. fake b.		fake	X
4.	fraud	X		
5.	honesty	X		
6.	impersonation		X	X
7.	motive			X

2 Rewrite the sentences by replacing the underlined word with the form in parentheses. Make any necessary grammatical changes.

1. I believe in the <u>honesty</u> of most doctors. (honest)

   I believe that most doctors are honest.

2. I had a bad experience with a man who practiced medicine <u>fraudulently</u>. (fraudulent)

   _____

3. His <u>motive</u> was making money. (motivate)

   _____

4. Not many people understood his <u>fakery</u>. (fake *n.*)

   _____

5. I wasn't the only person involved in his <u>deception</u>. (deceive)

   _____

6. He wasn't a real doctor, but he <u>impersonated</u> one well. (impersonation)

   _____

7. He had <u>duplicated</u> someone else's medical license. (duplicate *n.*)

   _____

CREATE

Imagine that you spent a lot of money on a fraudulent product or service. Write a letter to other customers, warning them about your bad experience. Use five new words.

GO TO MyEnglishLab FOR MORE VOCABULARY PRACTICE.

GRAMMAR

1 Read these sentences based on Frank Abagnale's story. Look at the boldfaced verbs. What is the difference between the verb forms? Notice the words in italics. How are the meanings of **when** and **while** different?

- Frank Abagnale **was hiding** in France *when* a flight attendant **reported** him to the authorities.

- *When* he **met** the doctor who helped him, they **were** both **renting** apartments in the same community.

- *While* the FBI **was searching** for him, he **was enjoying** himself in California.

SIMPLE PAST AND PAST PROGRESSIVE

1. Use the **simple past** tense to talk about actions, states, and situations in the past that take place at one point in time. The simple past tense of regular verbs is formed by adding **-d** or **-ed** to the base form of the verb.	He finally **passed** the law exam.
2. Use the **past progressive**, also called **past continuous**, to describe a continuous nonstop action that was in progress at a specific time in the past. Examples of specific time expressions include: *yesterday, last night, at that time.* The past progressive is formed like this: **be** (past) + **verb** + **-ing**.	*At that time*, he **was working** at a law firm.
3. Use the **past progressive** with the **simple past** tense to talk about an action that was interrupted by another action. Use the **simple past tense** for the interrupting action. Use **when** to introduce the simple past tense action.	He **was living** in France *when* a flight attendant **saw** him.
4. Use the **past progressive** with *while* to describe two actions in progress at the same time in the past. The **simple past** can also be used in the *while* clause without changing the meaning.	He **was enjoying** himself in California *while* the FBI **was searching** for him. He **was enjoying** himself in California *while* the FBI **searched** for him.
5. If you put the **when or while** clause first, you must put a **comma** at the end of the clause.	*When* the flight attendant **saw** him, he **was living** in France.

2 Complete the sentences with the correct form of the words in parentheses. Use the **simple past** or **past progressive**. Add a comma when necessary.

1. I was living in a new town when ___*I learned about a case of check fraud.*___
   (I / learn about a case of check fraud)

2. First, two men knocked on all the doors in my neighborhood while _____
   _____
   (my neighbors / relax at home on Sunday)

3. The men offered to do gardening work when _____
   _____
   (my neighbors /answer their door)

4. Next, the men asked my neighbors to write checks for $50 to their company, CAS. The
   men added an "H" to the checks when _____
   _____
   (they / take the checks to the bank)

Note: In the United States, it is sometimes possible to
get cash in exchange for checks that have *cash* written
on them instead of a person's name.

5. The two men were stealing a lot of money when
   _____
   _____
   (a bank clerk / finally become suspicious of what they / do)

6. When the clerk called the police _____
   _____
   (the police / arrest the two men)

7. I learned about this fraud while _____
   _____
   (I / watch the news on TV)

3 Think about the last time you became suspicious of something a person was doing. What
were you doing? What was the other person doing? On a separate piece of paper, write
two sentences with **while** and two sentences with **when**. Use simple past and past
progressive. Use commas when necessary.

GO TO MyEnglishLab *FOR MORE GRAMMAR PRACTICE AND TO CHECK WHAT YOU LEARNED.*

FINAL WRITING TASK

In this unit, you read about different kinds of fraud: impersonation, check fraud, and identity theft.

Now you are going to **write a paragraph describing an experience with fraud, yours or that of someone you know**. Use the vocabulary and grammar from the unit.*

PREPARE TO WRITE: Answering Questions

Think about an experience that you or a friend had with fraud. Answer the questions.

1. What happened?

_____

_____

2. What made it a fraud?

_____

_____

3. What were the consequences?

_____

_____

4. How did you or the other person feel after this experience? Why?

_____

_____

---

* For Alternative Writing Topics, see page 46. These topics can be used in place of the writing topic for this unit or as homework. The alternative topics relate to the theme of the unit but may not target the same grammar or rhetorical structures taught in the unit.

WRITE: A Story

When you **describe an experience**, you are **telling a story** about **something that happened** to you or someone else.

1 Read the paragraph and answer the questions.

> When my friend went to a car repair service, it was the worst experience of his life. He went there for a simple oil change. He was getting ready to go on a 200-mile trip to Boston, and he wanted to be sure his car was in good shape. The mechanic checked his engine and said the car needed much more than an oil change. He told him that it needed $1,000 worth of other repairs. My friend decided to let him do all the repairs because he was concerned about his trip. The mechanic charged him a total of $1,200 when he was finished with everything. A few hours later, my friend's car suddenly broke down while he was driving to Boston. He went to another car repair service, and they told him that his engine was now broken because of the other mechanic. He had to pay $1,500 for more repair. Now he had no more money left for his trip to Boston. He was very angry, so he decided to return to the first mechanic and ask for his money back. When he arrived at the car shop, it was closed. The mechanic had moved to another town, and my friend never saw him again.

1. What is the topic sentence of this paragraph?

_____

_____

2. How does the writer support the topic sentence?

_____

_____

_____

_____

_____

_____

WRITING A PARAGRAPH TO TELL A STORY

When writing a paragraph to **describe an experience** or **tell a story**, it is important to begin with a clear **topic sentence** that tells **what kind of experience** it was. The **following sentences** tell **what happened**. They include details that support the idea of the topic sentence. The **concluding sentence** tells **what happened at the end**. Look at the following examples:

- **Topic sentence:**
  When my friend went to a car repair service, it was the worst experience of his life.
- **What happened first:**
  He wanted to get ready for a trip and paid $1,200 for car repair.
- **What happened next:**
  His car broke down and he had to pay another $1,500 for more repair.
- **What happened next:**
  He stopped his trip and decided to get some of his money back.
- **Concluding sentence:**
  The mechanic had moved to another town, and my friend never saw him again.

2 Discuss the questions.

1. What kind of experience was this? What idea is expressed in the topic sentence?

2. How do the following sentences support this idea? Do they include positive or negative details?

3. What happened at the end? How is the concluding sentence related to the topic sentence?

3 Look at your answers from Prepare to Write, page 40. In one sentence, explain what kind of experience you had. This will be the topic sentence of your paragraph.

Example

  My brother had a very embarrassing experience with a con man.

4 Write the first draft of your paragraph. Tell what happened and include only details that support your topic sentence. Write a concluding sentence that tells what happened at the end. Don't worry too much about grammar while you write—just concentrate on describing the experience clearly.

REVISE: Using a Topic Sentence to Focus Ideas

A paragraph telling a story needs to have one main idea. This main idea is expressed in the topic sentence. **A good topic sentence is clear**. It helps the reader to **focus on the main idea**.

1 Read the paragraphs. Underline the topic sentences.

My sister wasted a lot of money on a fraudulent weight loss product. She saw an ad on TV for a special kind of tea. The ad promised that people who drink the tea lose weight very quickly. When she ordered the tea, she learned that she had to buy a six-month supply of the tea. This cost her $200. Unfortunately, the tea tasted terrible and it made her sick. She wasted $200 on a product that didn't work at all.

I had a bad experience with a dentist who promised to make my teeth look white. First, he charged me $800 for the tooth-whitening service. After I paid for the service, he told me that I couldn't drink coffee any more. I stopped drinking coffee for two days, and then I wanted to start drinking it again. As soon as I drank coffee, my teeth lost their new, white look. This was a very bad experience for me, and I'm still angry about it.

2 Choose the best topic sentence for these paragraphs. Circle the letter of your choice. Compare your answers with a partner's.

1. _____. She was looking for a job, and she found a website for people who work at home. The website said she could make $8,000 a month running a home business. She sent an email to the man in charge of the website. He told her to send him a check for $100 for special training software. She sent him the check but never heard from him again. When she looked for the website again, it was gone.
   a. My friend wanted to make $8,000 a month.
   b. My friend was cheated by an Internet con man.
   c. My friend was angry because she was cheated.

2. _____. It started when I left a magazine at the gym. It had my name and address on it. Somebody found the magazine and used my name and address to open a credit card. Soon, I started receiving bills for new clothes, furniture, and a trip to Hawaii. My bank didn't help me. My credit was ruined. I couldn't sleep or eat, and I started having problems at work because of the stress.
   a. I experienced identity theft at the gym.
   b. I had a terrible experience because of a magazine.
   c. My experience with identity theft almost destroyed my life.

3. _____. She had terrible back pain, and he told her that she needed to change her bed. He offered her a special deal on a new bed, and she bought it. When her back pain continued, he told her that she didn't need the bed at all. She needed to buy some vitamins from him. He told her to take two vitamins a day during the week and three vitamins a day on weekends. She didn't understand his advice at all.

    a. My sister was confused by the advice of a fraudulent doctor.

    b. My sister was angry because of the advice of a fraudulent doctor.

    c. My sister still had back pain after seeing a fraudulent doctor.

3 The topic sentences in these paragraphs are not clear. They do not help the reader to focus on the main idea. Read each paragraph. Then rewrite the topic sentence so that it is clear and focused.

1. Once I bought some new face cream. I wanted to look younger, and I thought the face cream would help me. But I couldn't find it anywhere. I tried four different stores in my city. Finally, I drove to another city. I got stuck in traffic for almost two hours. When I finally arrived at the store, it was closed. I went back the next week and bought the face cream. But it didn't work at all!

New topic sentence: _____

2. We are all human, and we all make mistakes. Last year, I used a credit card to buy some language learning CDs. The salesman promised that I could learn three different languages while I slept. Unfortunately, I learned nothing. I tried to return the CDs, but I couldn't get my money back. It took me several months to pay for them, and I really regret buying the CDs.

New topic sentence: _____

3. My uncle bought a fraudulent hair product. He has been bald for a long time. Last year, he saw an ad for a new hair product on TV. My uncle bought the product and used it right away. Then he went to a party and noticed that people were laughing at him. He looked in a mirror and saw that his bald head was turning blue. He tried washing off the color, but nothing worked.

New topic sentence: _____

4 Now go back to the first draft of your paragraph. Is the topic sentence clear and focused? Does the rest of the information in your paragraph support the topic sentence?

GO TO MyEnglishLab FOR MORE SKILL PRACTICE.

Go to MyEnglishLab and write the final draft of your paragraph. Carefully edit it for grammatical and mechanical errors, such as spelling, capitalization, and punctuation. Make sure you use some of the vocabulary and grammar from the unit. Use the checklist to help you write your final draft. Then submit your paragraph to your teacher.

FINAL DRAFT CHECKLIST

❏ Is your topic sentence clear and focused?

❏ Are all the supporting details related to the topic sentence?

❏ Does your paragraph clearly describe what happened in the experience?

❏ Does the concluding sentence explain what happened at the end?

❏ Are the simple past and past progressive verbs used correctly?

❏ Do you use new vocabulary from the unit?

❏ Is your paragraph formatted correctly?

UNIT PROJECT

Work in a small group. Go online and research recent cases of fraud. Compare your findings and write a report (one paragraph). Follow these steps:

STEP 1: Choose one of these types of fraud:

- Internet fraud
- medical fraud
- identity theft
- (*your own idea*)

STEP 2: Read two or more articles describing one recent case of fraud. Answer these questions:

- When did this fraud take place?
- What happened?
- How many people were involved?
- What were the financial consequences?
- What were the emotional and psychological consequences?

Work in a small group to compare your findings. Prepare a short report (one paragraph) for the class.

ALTERNATIVE WRITING TOPICS

Write about one of the topics. Use the vocabulary and grammar from the unit.

1. Write a paragraph describing the main characteristics of a con man or woman. What are some things that most con men or women have in common?

2. How can you protect yourself against identity theft or Internet fraud? What can you do? What can banks and other organizations do? Write a paragraph explaining your ideas.

3. In this unit you read about different types of fraud. Now write a paragraph giving some new examples of how technology has increased the dangers of fraud in our world today.

GO TO MyEnglishLab *TO WRITE ABOUT ONE OF THE ALTERNATIVE TOPICS, WATCH A VIDEO ABOUT IDENTITY THEFT, AND TAKE THE UNIT 2 ACHIEVEMENT TEST.*

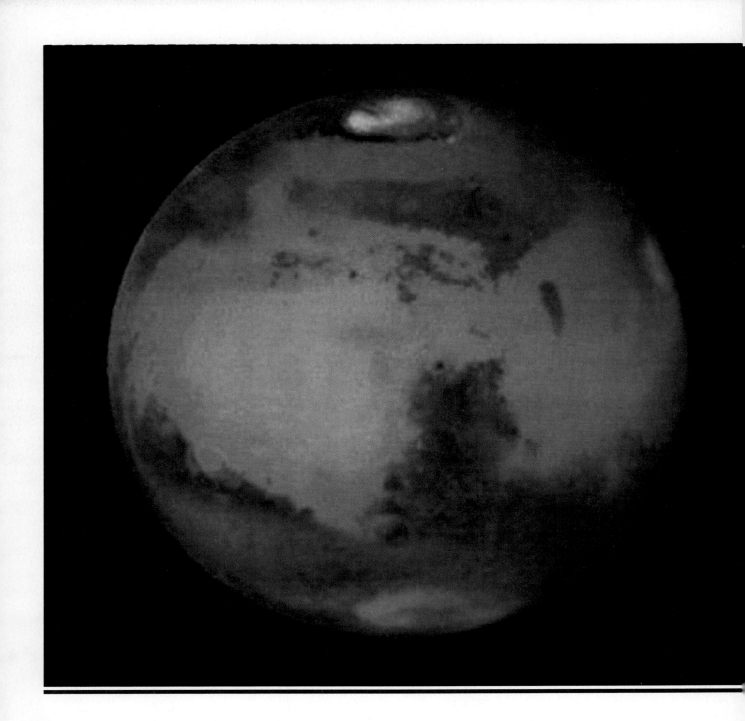

EXPLORING THE RED Planet

1 FOCUS ON THE TOPIC

1. When you were a child, did you ever look up in the night sky? What questions did you ask?

2. Exploring space costs a lot of money. Do you think what we learn is worth the cost?

3. What do you know about Mars? Do you know of any plans to explore Mars?

GO TO MyEnglishLab TO CHECK WHAT YOU KNOW.

VOCABULARY

1 Read this online article about a family living on Mars time. Pay attention to the boldfaced words.

ONE FAMILY'S "VACATION" TO MARS

When the Curiosity rover[1] landed on Mars in August of 2012, many of the mission's scientists on Earth decided to live on Mars time for the first 90 days of the mission. They had learned from earlier Mars missions that it is upsetting to their ability to sleep well when they are on Earth time at home and on Mars time at work. And they know that lack of sleep can lead to **depression**.

Curiosity exploring Mars

Such stress does not allow them to keep working. In addition, by changing their schedules to Mars time and **simulating** Martian days on Earth, they are able to control the actions of Curiosity from Earth when Curiosity is facing Earth. The Earth takes 24 hours to **spin** around once, but Mars takes 24 hours and 40 minutes. Mars time quickly becomes different from an Earth day. For example, in two and a half weeks, noon on Mars becomes 4:00 A.M. on Earth. The NASA scientists knew it would be a challenge to live and work on Mars time for 90 days; in fact, some of them didn't succeed in making the difficult change in their schedules. Those scientists that didn't **survive** the 90 days said they felt **isolated** from their families because they rarely saw them.

David Oh, the Curiosity mission's head scientist, knew being separated from his family would be difficult for him. He knew that he would miss them very much even though they would be living in the same house. He was **counting**

---

[1]**rover:** a vehicle that can be moved around

on three months of loneliness, but his family surprised him. For a month before school started, his wife and three children lived on Mars time with him. At first, he and his family thought that they would have a month of **boredom** because there would be nothing to do. Their (on Earth) **artificial** 24-hour-and-40-minute day would not offer a lot of activities for a young family of five. But soon they found a lot to do: bowling, eating at all-night diners, walking on the beach in moonlight, and seeing meteors[2] when the moon was not bright. They also cooked together, ate together, and watched movies together. David and his wife Bryn were most surprised by their children's **reaction**: they loved it and want to have another "vacation" to Mars during their next break from school!

[2]**meteor:** a small piece of rock that produces a bright line in the sky when it falls from space

2 Match the boldfaced words on the left with the definitions on the right.

___i___ **1. depression**   **a.** separate from others

_____ **2. simulate**   **b.** to make something look, sound, or feel like something else

_____ **3. spin**   **c.** to judge to be probable

_____ **4. survive**   **d.** to turn around and around quickly

_____ **5. isolated**   **e.** the feeling you have when you don't have anything to do

_____ **6. count on**   **f.** not real or natural, but made by people

_____ **7. boredom**   **g.** something that you feel or do because of something that has happened or been said

_____ **8. artificial**

_____ **9. reaction**   **h.** to continue to live normally in spite of difficulties

                               i. ~~being so sad and upset that you are unable to do anything~~

GO TO MyEnglishLab FOR MORE VOCABULARY PRACTICE.

Look at the title of the reading. Make a list of questions that you think will be answered in this reading.

1. _____

2. _____

3. _____

4. _____

5. _____

6. _____

Now read the article about Mars.

MARS: OUR NEW HOME?

1   If you think you'd like to live on Mars, you may have that possibility by 2023. A Dutch company called Mars One will soon advertise for people interested in colonizing[1] Mars. If you have all the necessary skills—and there are a lot—you could be one of the first colonists to Mars. Are you ready for the challenge?

2   Luckily, you won't have to find the money to pay for a mission to Mars because it would cost billions of dollars. Mars One has already received money from companies and some private donors.[2] It is also **counting on** getting money from everyday people who become interested in the television show they are planning to start soon. The show will follow teams of four applicants as they complete difficult jobs in difficult situations. The audience will vote for the best six teams. This show will be shown worldwide on television and on the Internet. Mars One is hoping that people will become so interested in the mission that they will give small and large amounts of money. Or at least buy a t-shirt—which Mars One already has available on its website.

3   As a future colonist in one of the six teams, you will go through years of training. If your team is the first team to travel to Mars, your main responsibility when you get there will be to build a place where humans can live. The atmosphere on Mars does not have enough

---

[1] **colonize:** to control an area and send your own people there to live

[2] **donor:** someone who gives something, especially money, to an organization

oxygen[3] for humans, and the land is not good enough to grow food. Colonists will have to create an **artificial** environment on Mars where there is air to breathe and land to farm. Scientists know Earth-like conditions can be **simulated** on Mars because something similar has already been done in Antarctica, where humans cannot **survive** outside the created environment.

4   Humans may have another problem in space as well. It takes nearly a year to get to Mars, so travelers would be without the Earth's gravity[4] for a long time. In addition, Mars One astronauts will not return to Earth. Their mission is to start a colony that can support itself. So, the colonists will live the rest of their lives there. When a human lives in an environment without gravity or with low gravity[5] for a long time, the systems in the body weaken. For example, muscles and bones lose strength. The heart also gets weaker. The blood in the body gets thicker, and it becomes more difficult for the heart to push blood through the body. Luckily, **spinning** the spaceship can create artificial gravity, and artificial gravity can ease these problems.

5   It also will be difficult for Mars colonists to be **isolated**, far from home, living in small spaces, and seeing the same people over and over. It is important to come up with solutions to possible problems before anyone actually goes on a Mars mission. Colonists with **depression** could put the mission in danger. Fortunately, a few years ago, a joint Russian and European project called the Mars500 Mission took place. It studied people's **reactions** to long-term space travel by following six astronauts in a Mars-like environment. The astronauts spent 520 days in this environment and only had contact with their bosses and their families. The six astronauts "returned" to the Earth in good physical condition—and still talking to each other. Scientists viewed the Mars500 Mission as a great success because they were able to see how the astronauts handle emotional and physical stresses. Surprisingly, the greatest emotional problem was **boredom**. The greatest physical problems were not getting enough sleep and gaining too much weight.

6   Recent polls show that seven percent of people would want to go on such an adventure. Mars One will soon start accepting applications for colonists. Applicants do not have to have any specific training, but they must be interested in learning new things and capable of solving problems. They also should be able to trust others and complete an assignment without stopping. Interested?

---

[3] **oxygen:** a gas in the air that has no color, smell, or taste. All living things need it in order to survive.

[4] **gravity:** the force that makes items fall to the ground

[5] **low gravity:** the gravity on Mars is only 38 percent of Earth's gravity

MAIN IDEAS

1   Look again at the Preview on page 51. How did your questions help you understand the reading?

2   Read each restatement of a main idea of the reading. In which paragraph is that main idea discussed? Write the paragraph number on the line on the next page. Then underline the main idea sentence in the paragraph.

(continued on next page)

_____ **a.** Ways to avoid feeling alone with only three other people, without a home, and in areas without much space must be found before going to Mars.

_____ **b.** Colonists will have to make Mars a place where they can live.

_____ **c.** A TV show will help raise money for the mission.

_____ **d.** The human body needs gravity to stay strong.

DETAILS

Circle the letter of the correct answer.

1. Which step is NOT part of the application process?

   a. Choose your team of four.

   b. Participate in challenging activities.

   c. Be on worldwide television.

2. How many teams of colonists will be trained to go to Mars?

   a. Four

   b. Five

   c. Six

3. What body parts get weaker in lower gravity?

   a. Brain

   b. Bones

   c. Lungs

4. When the Mars500 astronauts returned to Earth, they were _____.

   a. angry at each other

   b. heavier than they were before they left

   c. bored

5. What can colonists expect when they move to Mars?

   a. To be without Earth's gravity

   b. To have an emotional breakdown

   c. To pay for the trip

MAKE INFERENCES

INFERRING DEGREE OF DIFFICULTY

An **inference** is an **educated guess** about something that is **not directly stated** in a text. Writers sometimes **suggest degrees of difficulty** without stating them explicitly. A strong reader can **infer** these **degrees of difficulty** by reading the text closely.

Look at the example and read the explanation.

• Considering the cost of the mission to Mars, how difficult will it be for people to join?

Circle the best answer.

a. not so difficult

b. somewhat difficult

c. difficult

d. very difficult

(The best answer is a.)

In **paragraph 2**, we learn that colonists will not have to pay for their trip. Companies and private donors will supply the money for this mission.

After reading the text closely, we can **infer** that in terms of cost, joining the mission **won't be so difficult** since people won't have to pay anything.

Circle the best answer for each of the challenges the colonists will face in the Mars mission. Refer to the paragraphs in parentheses.

1. How difficult will it be to create an artificial environment? *(paragraph 3)*

   a. not so difficult

   b. somewhat difficult

   c. difficult

   d. very difficult

2. How difficult will it be to live without or with low gravity? *(paragraph 4)*

   a. not so difficult

   b. somewhat difficult

   c. difficult

   d. very difficult

(continued on next page)

3. How difficult will it be to deal with feelings of isolation? *(paragraph 5)*

   a. not so difficult
   b. somewhat difficult
   c. difficult
   d. very difficult

4. How difficult will it be to prevent boredom? *(paragraph 5)*

   a. not so difficult

   b. somewhat difficult

   c. difficult

   d. very difficult

Now discuss your answers with a partner. Point out sentences, words, or phrases in the paragraphs that helped you find the answers.

EXPRESS OPINIONS

Work in groups of three. Choose one of the questions. Discuss your ideas. Then choose one person in your group to report the ideas to the class.

1. MarsOne has begun a very grand project. Do you think that the mission will take place? By 2023? Why or why not?

2. Scientists believe that the information they learned from the Mars 500 project was valuable in understanding what colonists to Mars might have to face. Do you agree? Why or why not?

3. Would you want to join the Mars mission? Why or why not?

GO TO MyEnglishLab TO GIVE YOUR OPINION ABOUT ANOTHER QUESTION.

READ

1 Look at the boldfaced words in the reading and think about the questions.

1. Which words do you know the meaning of?

2. Can you use any of the words in a sentence?

2 Now read the online article about a timeline for going to Mars.

Timeline for a Mission to Mars

NASA currently has three spaceships orbiting[1] Mars and three rovers and one science lab on the planet, but they don't have plans to send colonists there like Mars One does. Sending anyone—colonists for the rest of their lives or astronauts for two months—to Mars takes a lot of planning. Space researchers have suggested plans for sending people to Mars, and their plans are based on real facts. But since no one has ever gone to Mars, their plans are only **speculations**. For example, the people at TV's Discovery Channel made a movie called *Race to Mars*, which follows a realistic timeline. The magazine *Popular Science* has also written about the steps needed to go to Mars. What timeline events can scientists agree on? Here is a plan that might be proposed.

Days 1–97   **Launching[2] Spaceships**
Parts for the three supply ships and one passenger ship are launched and begin to orbit the Earth. Spaceship builders put the ships together. After that, the three supply ships leave for Mars. The passenger ship waits in orbit until the astronauts arrive.

Days 98–112   **Checking the Health of the Astronauts**
The astronauts stay away from other people for two weeks before leaving Earth to avoid getting sick. Doctors make sure they are in good health.

---

[1] **orbit:** to move around a planet while in space
[2] **launch:** to send a ship into the sky or into space

(continued on next page)

Days 113–115 **Launching the Astronauts**
The astronauts leave Earth in the fifth ship and meet the passenger ship already in orbit. The ship connects to the passenger ship. The astronauts enter the passenger ship and make sure everything is in good working order.

Day 116 **Leaving Earth**
The **engines** fire to help the passenger ship leave the Earth's gravity. When the ship is in space, it begins to spin around. The spinning creates artificial gravity.

Daily Schedule for Trip to Mars	
07:00	Light comes on slowly
07:30	Breakfast
08:00–12:00	Work period (maintaining ship's systems)
12:15	Lunch
12:45–14:30	Free time (exercise, read, contact people on Earth, practice hobbies)
14:30–17:30	Work period
17:30–18:30	Exercise period
18:45	Dinner
19:30–22:00	Free time
22:30	Light begins to fade
23:00	Lights out

Days 116–356 **Traveling to Mars**
The trip to Mars takes 240 days. The schedule for each day is similar to a typical Earth day. *(See inset.)*

Day 342 **Reaching Mars: Supply Ships**
The supply ships arrive almost two weeks before the passenger ship does. After these ships are in orbit around Mars, two of the ships land on the surface. Because of their programming on Earth, the ships begin to work **automatically**. One of the supply ships is the artificial habitat, and it needs to be **established** in an appropriate area. The area needs to be large enough for the astronauts to do their **research** and prepare their experiments. The third ship waits in orbit for the passenger ship to arrive.

Day 356 **Reaching Mars: Passenger Ship**
After the passenger ship stops spinning, it enters orbit around Mars. It connects to the third supply ship. Then, the astronauts land on Mars. The passenger ship stays in orbit.

Day 357 **Beginning Mission**
The astronauts move into the artificial habitat, which supplies oxygen but not full gravity. They begin their exploration of Mars, which includes drilling for water, collecting rocks, and doing experiments to determine if there was ever life on Mars.

Day 417 **Leaving Mars**
The astronauts take off from Mars and connect to the passenger ship. They check the ship, get it ready, and begin their return to Earth.

Day 657 **Landing on Earth**
The astronauts get into the small ship and land on Earth in the ocean.

COMPREHENSION

Answer the questions. Discuss your answers with a partner.

1. How long are astronauts isolated from other people before they leave Earth? Why are they isolated?

2. On Day 116, why are the engines fired?

3. How is gravity made in space, where there is no gravity?

4. Which ship(s) arrive first at Mars? Why?

5. How many work hours are there in the daily schedule during the trip to Mars?

GO TO MyEnglishLab FOR MORE VOCABULARY PRACTICE.

READING SKILL

1 Look at Reading Two again. When you looked for the boldfaced words, did you read quickly or carefully?

SCANNING FOR DETAILS

Scanning is a useful skill that allows you to **find information quickly** without having to read the entire text. Before you carefully read Reading Two, you were asked to look at the boldfaced words. That was scanning.

In addition to **highlighted words**, you can scan for **key words, names,** or **numbers**. Key words are words that are often repeated. Look for capital letters when you want to find a name. Numbers are easy to find.

Scanning is very **useful when taking tests**, too. First read the question, and then scan the reading for the answer.

QUESTION: How many points are listed on this timeline?
(SCAN: *Count the number of underlined subheadings in the reading.*)

ANSWER: 10

QUESTION: Who made the movie *Race to Mars*?
(SCAN: *Find the title of the movie in italics and read around it.*)

ANSWER: The Discovery Channel

QUESTION: What happens on Day 417?
(SCAN: *Find that number on the list and just read what happens that day*).

ANSWER: The astronauts leave Mars.

2 Work with a partner. Scan Reading Two for the answers to these questions. Refer to the paragraphs or day numbers in parentheses.

1. How many NASA rovers are on Mars? How many ships orbit the planet? *(paragraph 1)*

2. What is *Popular Science*? *(paragraph 1)*

3. How many supply ships are necessary for a mission to Mars? *(Days 1–90)*

4. How long do the astronauts have to stay away from people before they leave for Mars? *(Days 98–112)*

5. How many days does it take to reach Mars? *(Days 116–356)*

GO TO MyEnglishLab FOR MORE SKILL PRACTICE.

CONNECT THE READINGS

STEP 1: Organize

Reading One (**R1**) and Reading Two (**R2**) contain information about Mars missions. Using this information, fill in the missing information in the chart. If there isn't a solution offered in Reading Two for a problem from Reading One, leave the cell blank.

PROBLEM (R1)	SOLUTION (R2)
1. *Lack of oxygen in Mars atmosphere*	Artificial habitat where oxygen in air is regulated
2. Poor soil on Mars	
3. Weak muscles, bones, and heart without gravity	
4. Feelings of isolation from home	
5. Boredom	
6.	Keeping busy with activity cause tiredness and sleep
7.	Required exercise periods

STEP 2: Synthesize

Imagine an informational interview between a Mars One representative and a woman interested in going to Mars as a colonist. Fill in the missing parts with information from the chart in Step 1.

MARS ONE: What questions do you have?

WOMAN: I've heard that the absence of gravity can cause physical problems. What kinds of physical problems?

MARS ONE: _____

WOMAN: Do you have solutions for these problems?

MARS ONE: Yes. Artificial gravity can be created in space by spinning the ship.

WOMAN: _____

MARS ONE: We're working on a way to create gravity on the planet. We should have a solution by the time the colonists leave for Mars.

WOMAN: What other problems will colonists face?

MARS ONE: _____. But there are solutions to these problems.

WOMAN: Such as?

MARS ONE: You will be very busy, so _____, and you'll be very tired by the end of the day, too.

WOMAN: So, I will sleep well. What about weight gain?

MARS ONE: _____

WOMAN: One more question: Will I ever be able to contact my friends on Earth? I think I would feel very lonely if I only had three other people to talk to.

MARS ONE: Yes, you will be able to talk to your friends on Earth. We don't want you to _____. Also, remember that there will be four new people arriving every year.

WOMAN: Thanks for your time. You've given me a lot to think about.

GO TO MyEnglishLab TO CHECK WHAT YOU LEARNED.

VOCABULARY

REVIEW

Complete the crossword puzzle. Read the clues and choose words from the box.

artificial	engines	simulate
automatically	establish	speculation
boredom	isolated	spin
count on	reaction	survive
depression	research	

Across

2. Small cells deep in the rock on Mars have been found, but they must be
   _____ from the rock in order to study them.

5. When there is a problem with Curiosity, a message is _____ sent to Earth.

8. There has been _____ about life on Mars for a long time.

9. For any living thing to _____ on Mars, there needs to be water.

10. Mars One will develop habitats on Mars that _____ the habitats in Antarctica.

13. As in previous Mars missions, scientists _____ _____ the rovers to collect
    rocks.

Down

1. What would your _____ be if life were discovered on Mars?

3. Without enough sleep, the astronauts may develop _____.

4. Without _____, rovers cannot move around on the surface of Mars.

6. _____ suggests that life on Mars may have been possible thousands of years
   ago.

7. _____ isn't a problem if you are studying the possibility of life on Mars.

10. Planets _____ around much more slowly than spaceships do.

11. _____ living space must be built on Mars in order for colonists to live there.

12. Scientists hope to _____ a Mars base in the future.

EXPAND

Fill in each blank with one of the words from the box. The missing word and the boldfaced
word make up an expression common in English.

artificial	automatic	establish	isolated	simulator

1. _____ **intelligence** is the science that allows computers to think and
   make decisions.

2. A **flight** _____ is a machine that makes you feel like you are flying, but
   you're really on the ground.

(continued on next page)

3. An _____ **incident** is an event that usually does not happen or that happened only once.

4. An _____ **pilot** system allows airplanes to fly themselves.

5. To _____ **yourself** is to do something that makes people notice you and take your skills seriously.

Write the five expressions. You will need them for the next activity.

_____   _____

_____   _____

_____

CREATE

Complete this journal entry by one of the future Mars colonists. Use three of the expressions you just learned and at least five new words from this unit.

Year 3, Day 1

I am just starting my third year of training to be a colonist to Mars, and I am really tired.

Sometimes, I don't know why I wanted to do this. _____.

_____

_____

_____

But, when I think about everything, _____

_____

_____

Lights out! I must go to bed now.

■■ *GO TO* MyEnglishLab *FOR MORE VOCABULARY PRACTICE.*

GRAMMAR

1 Read the sentences. Underline the verbs that have the form to + verb. What questions do these verbs answer?

- The engines fire to leave orbit.
- The mission was started to build a colony.
- The ship is spinning to create artificial gravity.

INFINITIVES OF PURPOSE	
Questions	Answers
Why do the engines fire?	They fire **to leave** Earth's orbit.
Why was the mission started?	It was started **to build** a colony on Mars.
Why is the ship spinning?	It is spinning **to create** artificial gravity.
1. Infinitives (*to* + **verb**) that are used to explain the purpose of an action are called **infinitives of purpose**. They answer the question *Why*?	The engines fire **to leave** Earth's orbit. The mission was started **to build** a colony on Mars. The ship is spinning **to create** artificial gravity.
2. You can also use the longer form *in order to* + **verb**.	The engines fire **in order to leave** Earth's orbit. The mission was started **in order to build** a colony on Mars. The ship is spinning **in order to create** artificial gravity.

2 Match the questions on the left with the answers on the right.

Questions	Answers
_____ 1. Why does MarsOne need to find money?	**a.** in order to avoid their getting sick
_____ 2. Why do planet builders need years?	**b.** to go to Mars
_____ 3. Why do the colonists use the radio?	**c.** in order to talk to their families on Earth
_____ 4. Why are the astronauts isolated before leaving on a trip to Mars?	**d.** to sleep well at night
_____ 5. Why does MarsOne have a selection committee?	**e.** in order to change the atmosphere of Mars
_____ 6. Why will colonists exercise a lot?	**f.** to choose four astronauts

3 Combine the questions and answers (from the previous activity) to make sentences that answer the questions "Why?"

1. _____ *MarsOne needs to find money to go to Mars.* _____

2. _____

3. _____

4. _____

5. _____

6. _____

■■■■■■■■■■■■■■■■■■ *GO TO* MyEnglishLab *FOR MORE GRAMMAR PRACTICE AND TO CHECK WHAT YOU LEARNED.*

FINAL WRITING TASK

In this unit, you read about a plan to build a colony on Mars. The job of colonist is open to anyone. Would you go on a Mars mission?

You are going to **write a paragraph answering this question and explaining your decision.** What are the pros and cons of deciding one way or the other? Evaluate your own abilities. Use the vocabulary and the grammar from this unit.*

PREPARE TO WRITE: Evaluating Pros and Cons

Fill in the chart with the pros and cons of going to Mars. Don't think too much. Just list any ideas that come into your mind.

PROS	CONS

---

* For Alternative Writing Topics, see page 72. These topics can be used in place of the writing topic for this unit or as homework. The alternative topics relate to the theme of the unit but may not target the same grammar or rhetorical structures taught in the unit.

An **outline** is a plan for how you will write a text. The following outline is for writing a **paragraph**. Use outlines to help organize the main idea and details that you want to include. Use your outline to organize your topic sentence, supporting points, supporting details, and concluding sentence.

> I. **Topic Sentence**
>
> II. **Supporting Point**
>
>   **A.** Supporting Detail
>
>   **B.** Supporting Detail
>
> III. **Supporting Point**
>
>   **A.** Supporting Detail
>
>   **B.** Supporting Detail
>
> IV. **Concluding Sentence**

1 Read this paragraph about a difficult decision. Then discuss the questions with a partner.

Which Mars Team Job to Take

After graduating, I chose a job at the Ames Research Center in Mountain View (near San Francisco) instead of the job at Jet Propulsion Laboratory in Pasadena (near Los Angeles) for three reasons. The first reason was emotional. Everyone in my family lives on the peninsula between San Francisco and San Jose, and I like to attend all the family get-togethers. And if I need help, I can count on them to help me. Moreover, my parents are both in their 70s, and I want to be able to help them as they get even older. Secondly, it is smoggy and hot in southern California, especially in the summer. I know this is true because I lived there for over 10 years. It is true that the air quality has improved a lot in the last 20 years, but it's not as good as the air in the Bay Area. The last reason I chose the job in northern California is that San Francisco has far fewer people than Los Angeles does. San Francisco's population is about 800,000, and Los Angeles' is about 3,500,000. San Francisco can't really grow because it is surrounded by water on three sides, but

(continued on next page)

Los Angeles can (and has) spread out a lot. Although I thought it would be difficult to choose between two dream jobs, it really wasn't because the area near the Ames Research Center is close to my family, has cleaner air, and is less crowded.

1. What choice was the writer faced with?

2. How many reasons did the writer give for the decision?

3. What were the reasons?

2 Complete the outline with information from the paragraph.

I. Topic Sentence: _After graduating, I chose a job at the Ames Research Center in_ _Mountain View (near San Francisco) instead of the job at Jet Propulsion Laboratory_ _in Pasadena (near Los Angeles) for three reasons._

II. Supporting Point: _The first reason was emotional._
Supporting Details: _I like to attend family get-togethers._
_____

III. Supporting Point: _____
Supporting Details: _____
_____

IV. Supporting Point: _____
Supporting Details: _____
_____

3 Look at your answers from Prepare to Write on page 66. Organize your ideas into an outline. Then use your outline to write the first draft of your paragraph. Be sure to include:

- **A topic sentence**

- **Two or three supporting points**. Each one should focus on the reasons for your decision. Then use details to explain each supporting point.

- **A concluding sentence** that summarizes your reasons.

1 Read the sentences about NASA jobs. Label the subjects and the verbs.

- Most people think you have to have an advanced degree to work at NASA, but many jobs do not require engineering or science degrees.
- NASA has locations in California, Texas, Louisiana, Florida, and Maryland.

PARALLEL STRUCTURE

Writers use **parallel structure** when they put two or three words or phrases of the same part of speech (noun, verb, adjective, adverb) together in sentences. The use of parallel structure allows writers to express several ideas in one sentence.

- NASA employees **plan space missions, study weather patterns, fix computers,** and **type letters**.
- NASA is looking for **intelligent, educated,** and **healthy** college graduates to work for them.

Two ideas can be expressed in one sentence:

- When I went online, I **found** the NASA job openings.
- When I went online, I **read** about the types of jobs I could do.
- When I went online, I **found** the NASA job openings and **read** about the types of jobs I could do.

A third idea can be added:

- When I went online, I **applied** for a job.
- When I went online, I **found** the NASA job openings, **read** about the types of jobs I could do, and **applied** for a job.
  *(Notice that **found, read,** and **applied** are all in the past tense.)*

Look at two more examples:

    [ADV] [V]   [ADV]   [V]
- I **easily filled** out the application and **successfully submitted** it.
  (The phrases are parallel because they both contain an adverb and a verb.)
           [ADJ]   [N]   [ADJ]   [N]
- I hope the job has a **good environment** and **friendly colleagues**.
  (The phrases are parallel because they both contain an adjective and a noun.)

2 Use parallel structure to combine each pair of sentences.

1. NASA treats its employees well.
   NASA pays its employees well.

   _____

2. NASA carefully reviews each candidate.
   NASA fairly reviews each candidate.

   _____

3. In college, I studied astronomy.
   In college, I studied geology.

   _____

4. On my first day at my new job, the boss was very helpful.
   On my first day at my new job, my coworkers were very helpful.

   _____

5. When the Curiosity rover landed on Mars, I went on Mars time.
   When the Curiosity rover landed on Mars, I didn't see my family very much.

   _____

6. NASA has safely launched many spaceships.
   NASA has proudly launched many spaceships.

   _____

7. I learned a lot during my first year at NASA.
   I made many friends during my first year at NASA.

   _____

3 Describe your dream job, a job you would like to have. Complete the paragraph.
Use parallel structure.

My Dream Job

I would like to work as a / an _____. This job is _____,

(name of the job)   (ADJ)

_____, and _____. People who do this job are talented because

(ADJ)   (ADJ)

they can _____ and _____. I respect these people because they

(V)   (V)

work so _____ and _____. I would like to have this job because of

(ADV)   (ADV)

its _____ _____ and _____ _____

(ADJ)   (N)   (ADJ)   (N)

.

4 Now go back to the first draft of your paragraph. Rewrite at least three to four
sentences using parallel structure.

GO TO MyEnglishLab *FOR MORE SKILL PRACTICE.*

EDIT: Writing the Final Draft

Go to MyEnglishLab and write the final draft of your paragraph. Carefully edit it for
grammatical and mechanical errors, such as spelling, capitalization, and punctuation. Make sure
you use some of the vocabulary and grammar from the unit. Use the checklist to help you
write your final draft. Then submit your paragraph to your teacher.

FINAL DRAFT CHECKLIST

❏ Does your paragraph clearly explain the reasons for your decision?

❏ Does it contain a topic sentence, two or three supporting points, and a
concluding sentence?

❏ Does each supporting point focus clearly on one reason?

❏ Are there details to explain each supporting point?

❏ Does the concluding sentence summarize the supporting points (the reasons)?

❏ Are infinitives of purpose used correctly?

❏ Does your paragraph use parallel structure?

❏ Do you use new vocabulary from the unit?

UNIT PROJECT

Work in a small group. Research other missions to Mars on the Internet. Write a report (one paragraph) about one. Share the report with your classmates. Follow these steps:

STEP 1: Choose one of NASA's Missions to Mars.

- Mars Exploration Rovers
- Mars Express
- Mars Global Surveyor
- Mars Odyssey
- Mars Pathfinder
- Mars Reconnaissance Orbiter
- Mars Science Laboratory

STEP 2: Find out information about the mission you chose. Some facts you may want to learn about:

- Purpose of mission
- Date launched
- Current location
- Current usefulness (Is it still active?)
- Future plans

STEP 3: Work with your group to prepare a short written report (one paragraph). Use the outline technique you learned in this unit to organize your report. Then orally summarize the report for the class.

ALTERNATIVE WRITING TOPICS

Write about one of the topics. Use the vocabulary and grammar from the unit.

1. Do you believe that there is life on other planets? If you do, what do you imagine it would be like? Write a paragraph describing it.

2. Mars One is privately funded, but other space programs like those in the United States are funded by taxpayer money. Do you think spending money on space programs is worth the money that is spent? Why or why not? Write a paragraph explaining your ideas.

3. Over 1,000 people have shown interest in applying for the one-way mission to Mars that Mars One is offering. What characteristics does a person need to go on such a mission? Write a paragraph describing that person.

■■■■■■■■■■■■■■■■■■■■■■■■■■ *GO TO* MyEnglishLab *TO WRITE ABOUT ONE OF THE ALTERNATIVE TOPICS, WATCH A VIDEO ABOUT SPACE, AND TAKE THE UNIT 3 ACHIEVEMENT TEST.* ■■■■■■■■■■■■■■■■■■■■■■■■■■

LANGUAGE AND Power

1 FOCUS ON THE TOPIC

1. Look at the photograph. How is it possible for people of different nationalities and cultures to communicate with each other?

2. Read the title of the unit. How do language and power relate to each other?

3. Can you tell a person's gender by the way he or she communicates? How do people of both genders use language to gain power?

GO TO MyEnglishLab *TO CHECK WHAT YOU KNOW.*

VOCABULARY

1 Read the description of a college course in linguistics, the scientific study of language and the use of language in societies. Pay attention to the boldfaced words.

LINGUISTICS 120

GENDER DIFFERENCES IN LANGUAGE

In this course, we will study how men and women use language differently. We will answer the following questions:

1. Gender is a basic part of identity. When we think about who we are, we begin by thinking of ourselves as male or female. How do we use language to communicate who we are and which things are most **valued** in our lives?

2. There are differences in the way that males and females use language. Is it true that men are more **assertive** than women and communicate more directly? Is it a **myth** that women use language more politely than men? Since the 1990s, it has become more acceptable for women to use **profanity**, but people still feel uncomfortable when this happens in mixed gender groups. Why?

3. Our home culture strongly affects our behavior. In our home culture, we learn how to act as males and females. We also learn how much talking is acceptable to others and how much is considered **excessive**. One way to understand a culture is to look at its **proverbs**, including those about language and gender. What do proverbs show us about a culture's way of thinking about males and females?

4. Is it possible to know the gender of a speaker just by listening to his or her speech? What about the idea that females are more **talkative** than males? Is this true or do males **dominate** more conversations and discussions at work and school?

5. All human beings want to be respected by others. They want others to admire them, and they want to feel important. What about **sexism**, the unfair treatment of women based on the belief that they are **inferior** to males? How does this affect our thinking about language and gender?

2 Match the boldfaced words on the left with the definitions on the right.

_e_   **1. assertive**   **a.** unfair treatment of women or men because of their gender

_____   **2. dominate**   **b.** honored and respected

_____   **3. excessive**   **c.** weaker or less important

_____   **4. inferior**   **d.** talking a lot

_____   **5. myth**   ~~**e.** strongly asking for what you want or need~~

_____   **6. profanity**   **f.** to exercise control over

_____   **7. proverb**   **g.** a belief that is untrue

_____   **8. sexism**   **h.** very rude or disrespectful language

_____   **9. talkative**   **i.** too much

_____   **10. valued**   **j.** a traditional saying

GO TO MyEnglishLab FOR MORE VOCABULARY PRACTICE.

PREVIEW

You are going to read a student's essay about men, women, and language. Read the first paragraph. Then complete these sentences with **men** or **women**, based on how you think the writer will answer the questions she asks in the first paragraph.

1. _____Men_____ joke more than _____women_____.

2. _____ speak more politely than _____.

3. _____ complain less than _____.

4. _____ gossip more than _____.

5. _____ ask for directions more often than _____.

Now read the whole essay.

Men, Women, and Language

1   Imagine a playground in the United States. A boy, Ashton, and a girl, Laney, are playing with other children. Will their games be the same? What about the ways they talk to each other? Will their use of language be the same? It's impossible to answer these questions without thinking about gender, the differences that we can see in the behavior of males and females. This behavior includes language use, the way that males and females use their words to communicate with others and to express themselves. As we examine the development of ideas on language and gender, it is important to consider how differences in male and female language show differences in power.

Late Twentieth-Century Research: Lakoff and Tannen

2   In the late twentieth century, two scholars,[1] Robin Lakoff and Deborah Tannen, developed important ideas on language and gender. Robin Lakoff described female speech in her book *Language and Woman's Place*. According to Lakoff, females are less **assertive** in their speech, avoiding jokes and **profanity**. Lakoff wrote her book in the 1970s, a time when scholars were examining the position of women in society. They were exploring the idea of **sexism**, the unfair treatment of women based on a view of them as **inferior**.

3   During the next two decades, Deborah Tannen wrote popular books such as *You Just Don't Understand* that made the public aware of important differences between male and female communication. Like Lakoff, Tannen agreed that women speak more politely and less directly than men. For instance, instead of ordering someone directly to open a door, a woman will often use a polite question, such as "Could you please open the door?"

Tannen identified female speech as RAPPORT TALK, which can be described as follows:

   • the use of language to build relationships with others
   • showing agreement with each other
   • discussion of weakness and fear

In contrast, Tannen described male speech as REPORT TALK, with the following characteristics:

   • the use of language to show your knowledge
   • avoiding personal topics
   • discussion of sports or politics

4   A well-known example used by Tannen to show differences in communication styles is that of a husband and wife who are lost and need directions. The wife will usually want to ask someone for directions, which involves admitting weakness and depending on someone's help. The husband, on the other hand, will usually prefer to use a map or GPS and solve the problem by himself. Both Lakoff and Tannen did important work to help us understand how men and women use language differently in the English-speaking world.

---

[1] **scholar:** a person who studies a subject at a very advanced level

Early Twenty-first-Century Research: Poole and Cameron

5   Now, in the twenty-first century, scholars continue to explore important ideas on language and gender. Jennifer Poole, author of *Women, Men and Language*, has looked closely at women's speech and divided it into categories, including these:

- HOUSE TALK: speech that is focused on sharing information related to women's traditional role of housekeeping
- SCANDAL: speech that is focused on criticizing other people's behavior and discussing whether it is right or wrong
- CHATTING: the sharing of personal information in a way that allows women to support and care for each other
- GRIPING: complaining to each other about their lives as women and their lack of freedom and independence

6   Like Tannen did earlier, Poole has focused on female speech as a way of building relationships with other people. For instance, as women chat about their lives, they share common feelings and help each other emotionally. The "scandal" talk described by Poole is similar to Tannen's description of female gossip, discussion of other people's secrets. Sharing gossip allows a girl or woman to prove that she is close enough to others to know private details about them.

7   Another scholar, Deborah Cameron, examines the differences in male and female language and questions where these differences come from. In contrast to the idea that speech differences are a natural part of gender, Cameron believes that they are based on the fact that men have more power than women in society. In her book *What Language Barrier?*, she disagrees with the idea that women talk more than men and asserts that men often **dominate** conversations. She views the idea that women talk more than men do as a negative opinion that women talk too much. This opinion is based on the sexist idea that women are less important than men.

The Traditional View and How It Is Changing

8   This brings us back to considering the place of women in society. For centuries, people around the world have said that women are too **talkative**. We can see this idea in several **proverbs**, including these:

- "A woman's tongue is her weapon,[2] and she does not let it rust.[3]" (*Chinese*)
- "It's an unhappy house where the hen[4] is louder than the rooster.[5]" (*French*)
- "A woman's hair is long, but her tongue is even longer." (*Russian*)

9   These proverbs show us the **myth** of the talkative woman, which is based on an unfair view of their inferiority. This view still exists in many societies even though the position of

(continued on next page)

---

[2] **weapon:** an object used to hurt others, such as a gun or knife
[3] **rust:** to turn a reddish-brown color, sometimes because of not being used
[4] **hen:** a female chicken
[5] **rooster:** a male chicken

women has greatly improved in the last century. When a person has social, political, and economic power, their speech is **valued**, not seen as **excessive**. As women gain power through education and employment, they may speak more directly and less politely, making more jokes instead of saying, "excuse me" and "I'm sorry." With more power in society, women might speak more like men. Likewise, as men share more power, they might speak more politely and dominate fewer conversations. As we look at ideas on language and gender, we see that speech is more than communication. It is an expression of power in many societies.

MAIN IDEAS

1 Look again at the Preview on page 77. How did your answers help you understand the essay?

2 Write **T** (true) or **F** (false) for each statement. Rewrite the false statements to make them true.

    _F_ **1.** Ideas on language and gender have ~~basically stayed the same~~ *changed* over the last 100 years.

    _____ **2.** According to Lakoff and Tannen, men use language more assertively than women.

    _____ **3.** Poole has divided male speech into four categories.

    _____ **4.** Poole and Tannen agree that female speech is focused on showing knowledge.

    _____ **5.** In Cameron's opinion, differences in language are based on differences in power.

    _____ **6.** Cameron believes that females are less talkative than males.

    _____ **7.** Proverbs from several cultures focus on how talkative men are.

    _____ **8.** Women may speak more assertively as they gain more power.

DETAILS

Circle the best answer for each question. Write the number of the paragraph where you found the answer.

1. What does sexism against women mean?   _2_

   a. avoiding profanity
   b. treating them unfairly
   c. using language assertively

2. How do women generally use language, according to Tannen?   _____

   a. They ask for things politely.
   b. They tell people what to do.
   c. They give direct orders.

3. What does "rapport talk" include doing?   _____

   a. discussing the news
   b. talking about weakness
   c. telling funny jokes

4. What is discussed in "report talk"?   _____

   a. complaints about people's behavior
   b. secrets and fears
   c. impersonal topics such as sports

5. According to Poole, what is the goal of female chatting?   _____

   a. to discuss new ways of cleaning house
   b. to give and receive emotional support
   c. to show knowledge

6. Why is gossip valuable to girls and women?   _____

   a. It is proof of having a close relationship with someone.
   b. It is a way to share secrets about someone else.
   c. It shows that one is more powerful than others.

(continued on next page)

7. How does Cameron think men and women behave in conversation? _____

    a. Men and women both dominate conversations.

    b. Men are less talkative than women.

    c. Men actually talk more than women.

8. What does the essay writer believe about "excessive" speech? _____

    a. It's related to having less power.

    b. It's related to having more power.

    c. It's related to having excessive power.

MAKE INFERENCES

INFERRING THE MEANINGS OF PROVERBS

An **inference** is an **educated guess** about something that is **not directly stated** in a text. Writers sometimes use **proverbs** as an interesting **way of suggesting an idea** without directly stating it. To understand a proverb, readers need to **go beyond the exact meaning of words** and think about other possible meanings.

Look at the example and read the explanation.

- "A woman's tongue is her weapon and she does not let it rust."

What does this proverb mean? Choose the best answer.

    a. Women hurt people with their words.

    b. Women have very dangerous tongues.

    c. Women argue constantly until they win.

(The best answer is c.)

We know that *tongue* can mean words or language because people use their tongues to speak. A *weapon* is used for fighting. Fighting with words is arguing. People who argue have a chance to get what they want. If a weapon is used constantly, it will not *rust* or get damaged and become useless. **Conclusion:** To get what they want, women talk and argue a lot.

After thinking carefully about the possible meaning of important words in the proverb, we have a better idea of what the whole proverb means. We **can infer** the **meaning of the proverb**.

Read each proverb. Think carefully about what important words in the proverb mean. Circle the best meaning of each proverb.

1. "It's an unhappy house where the hen is louder than the rooster."

   a. Men, not women, should control the family.
   b. Families are happy when women talk more than men.
   c. A happy family has a father who talks a lot.

2. "A woman's hair is long, but her tongue is even longer."

   a. Women with long hair talk a lot.
   b. Excessive talking is part of being a woman.
   c. Beautiful women speak too much.

Now discuss your answers with a partner. Explain why you chose each answer.

EXPRESS OPINIONS

Work in groups of three. Choose one of the questions. Discuss your ideas. Then choose one person in your group to report the ideas to the class.

1. Give an example of sexism in your home culture. It can be an example from school, work, business, or family.

2. Do you agree that men and women use language differently? If so, what do you think are the most noticeable differences between male and female use of language?

3. What is another myth that people believe about men or women? Can you think of any proverbs related to this myth?

■■■■■■■■■■■■■■■■■■■■■■■■■■■■■■■■■ GO TO MyEnglishLab *TO GIVE YOUR OPINION ABOUT ANOTHER QUESTION.*

READING TWO THE QUESTION OF GLOBAL ENGLISH

READ

1 Look at the boldfaced words in the reading on the next page and think about the questions.

   1. Which words or phrases do you know the meanings of?

   2. Can you use any of the words or phrases in a sentence?

2 Now read the *Traveling Man* blog, written by a traveler who is interested in different languages and cultures.

The Question of Global English

Traveling Man—**Jason C.**—July 17

1   Hello, fellow travelers.

I'm on my way to France through the Spanish Basque country. Last night I saw a big sign at a café reading: *English spoken here*. It got me thinking: is English as a global language helping people around the world to communicate better? Or is it causing us to lose our **uniqueness** and independence? Is it fair to have one powerful language that people around the world have to learn?

2   JOHN L: As an American, I like it. I can talk to people wherever I go and I don't have to learn any other languages. At the same time, I sometimes feel embarrassed when I compare myself to people who know English, plus two or three other languages. I feel so stupid sometimes.

3   MIGUEL F: Using English as a global language makes sense to me. It's convenient for us to have a common language. They tried Esperanto, but that didn't spread like English. Language can't be created or forced. It's a natural expression of a culture. As an invented language, Esperanto doesn't have any native culture.

4   JASON C: What's Esperanto? Isn't that some kind of spy language from World War II?

5   MIGUEL F: Earlier than that—it goes back to the 1880s. A scholar invented it to give people a common language they could all learn easily. He felt that having different languages divides people into enemy groups. He hoped that Esperanto would change things.

6   YI-WEN C: But the grammar of Esperanto is based on European languages, so it's not that easy for non-Europeans to learn. Besides, it's not as cool as speaking English. English is more than a language. It's an attitude, a lifestyle. It's Hollywood, rock and roll.

7   **VASILY Z:** It's all political. Whoever wins a war gets to control the language of the world. But I do agree that it's easier for people to have a common language. So why not English? It's a simple language. If it weren't that easy, how could a billion people around the world have learned it?

8   **YUKO H:** I don't think it's easy at all. It's taken me years to learn it.

9   **PAOLO B:** I agree. I hate how the spelling's so complicated, so full of exceptions.

10   **ASHOK P:** I like that it has so many **dialects**. You don't have to speak like any one nationality—you have choices.

11   **ALI M:** For me, it was easy to learn English at school in Qatar since I went to an English-speaking school. Now my English is almost perfect. And I started young, so it wasn't too hard to learn.

12   **YUKO H:** I wish I had perfect English. I'm not even close. There's so much **slang**, and so many **synonyms**—it gives me a headache. And why are there so many verb tenses? Do we really need to know the past perfect? Give me Esperanto.

13   **GORKA A:** Try learning Basque if you want a real challenge. English is so much easier!

14   **JASON C:** I'm not so sure now. Thanks for sharing your ideas. I'll post again as soon as I get to France.

COMPREHENSION

Read the statements and mark them **T** (true) or **F** (false). Rewrite the false statements to make them true.

_____ **1.** Most Americans speak several languages.

_____ **2.** Esperanto was invented as a language to help people find peace.

_____ **3.** There are one billion non-native speakers of English in the world.

_____ **4.** English can be difficult because of spelling, vocabulary, and grammar.

_____ **5.** Everyone agrees that English is a difficult language to learn.

GO TO MyEnglishLab *FOR MORE VOCABULARY PRACTICE.*

READING SKILL

1   In Reading Two, people express their opinions about English as a global language. A strong reader is able to understand how examples are used to support opinions.

UNDERSTANDING HOW EXAMPLES SUPPORT OPINIONS

Writers sometimes present a variety of opinions in a text. Readers need to understand how **different examples support different opinions.**

Look at these opinions and examples from Reading One:

OPINION 1: Tannen agrees that women speak more politely and less directly than men.
EXAMPLE 1: "For instance, instead of ordering someone directly to open a door, a woman will often use a polite question, such as, 'Could you please open the door?'"

OPINION 2: Poole looks at female speech as a way of building relationships with other people.
EXAMPLE 2: "Women chat about their lives, share common feelings, and help each other emotionally."

Again, it is important to read examples carefully and think about their meaning. Remember that the **purpose of an example is to support a main idea.**

2 Work with a partner. Read each opinion from Reading Two. Then match the opinion with a supporting example.

Opinions	Supporting Examples
<u> c </u> **1.** As an American, I like global English.	**a.** Basque
_____ **2.** The inventor of Esperanto believed in having a common language.	**b.** English
_____ **3.** Language is political.	~~**c.** Speakers of English don't have to learn other languages.~~
_____ **4.** A grammar based on European languages is difficult for non-Europeans to learn.	**d.** People who are divided by different languages often fight wars.
_____ **5.** A language is easy if billions of people can learn it.	**e.** The world's global language depends on the result of war.
_____ **6.** Some languages are more difficult than others.	**f.** Esperanto

GO TO MyEnglishLab FOR MORE SKILL PRACTICE.

CONNECT THE READINGS

STEP I: Organize

Reading One (**R1**) and Reading Two (**R2**) contain information about the relationship between language and power. Look at the list of beginning statements and write each one under the correct heading in the chart. Then complete each statement with important information from R1 or R2.

a. Women's speech is viewed as excessive because . . .

b. Native speakers of English don't have to . . .

c. One reason English has become a global language is because of . . .

d. If women had more power, they might speak . . .

e. One reason why women speak more politely than men is that . . .

f. People who speak English can communicate . . .

(continued on next page)

LANGUAGE AND GENDER (R1)	ENGLISH AS A GLOBAL LANGUAGE (R2)
1. *Women's speech is viewed as excessive because they are less valued than men.*	1.
2.	2.
3.	3.

STEP 2: Synthesize

Imagine that you are writing a paragraph in a linguistics class. Complete the paragraph outline with information from Step 1. Then use the outline to write a complete paragraph.

I. Topic Sentence: The use of language is an expression of power in individual societies and also between nations.

II. Supporting Point: In most societies, men have more power than women.

Supporting Details: **A.** Male speech = _____ than female speech

B. Female speech = _____ than male speech

C. The myth of the "talkative woman" is part of many societies because _____

_____.

III. Supporting Point: As a global language, English offers advantages as a tool of communication between nations.

Supporting Details: **A.** English has become a global language because of _____

_____.

B. Native speakers don't have to _____

_____.

C. Non-native speakers can _____

_____.

IV. Concluding Sentence: Language use is an expression of power both internationally and also within individual societies.

GO TO MyEnglishLab TO CHECK WHAT YOU LEARNED.

VOCABULARY

REVIEW

Read an email message from a non-native speaker of English. In this message to a friend, he describes a visit to his American wife's family. Complete the letter with words from the box. Use each word only once.

assertive	exception	myth	sexism	synonyms
~~dialect~~	excessive	profanity	slang	uniqueness
dominate	inferior	proverb	talkative	valued

○ ○ ○

Hi Pedro,

I finally have a few free minutes here in Seattle, where we're visiting Ashley's parents. Her two sisters,

Brooke and Lauren, are visiting them too, so I met the whole family.

It's amazing how her family is so different from mine. First of all, her older sister, Brooke, lives in

London and has picked up the local _____dialect_____. It hasn't been easy for me to communicate
                                         1.

with her. Her pronunciation is hard to understand, and so is the _____ that she uses
                                                                      2.

in casual conversation. I thought I knew a lot of English vocabulary, especially _____ ,
                                                                                    3.

but some of the words she uses have totally different meanings. (I thought a "boot" was a type of shoe,

but to Brooke, it's part of a car!) Another thing is that Brooke has a very strong personality. No matter

what we're talking about, she tries to _____ the conversation. I mentioned this to
                                          4.

Ashley, and she got mad at me for my _____. She thinks that men who complain about
                                          5.

_____ women are hanging on to the old idea that women are _____
        6.   7.

to men. Another difference is that her mom is a lot more _____ than mine. She owns a
                                                              8.

small company and is used to getting things done. After talking to her for a while, I think it's definitely a

_____ that women aren't strong enough for business. She's a very strong lady—
        9.

(continued on next page)

and I think that's part of the family's _____. I've never met a mother like this one
                                            10.

before. Also, I'm a bit shocked by Ashley's younger sister, Lauren. I'm not used to hearing so much

_____ from a female, but I guess it's her age. Maybe girls are freer to say what
          11.

they want to these days, and Lauren is no _____. Or maybe I was raised with
                                                12.

_____ politeness because of my old-fashioned parents. I don't know. Spending
       13.

time with Ashley's family reminds me of the old _____ that you don't just marry a
                                                       14.

person—you marry a person's family, too. Anyway, I've had a pretty good time with them. They seem

to like me and make me feel like a _____ part of the family.
                                          15.

I'll see you in a couple of days when we get back. You can check the pictures on my website.

Taka

EXPAND

1 Complete the chart with the correct word forms. Use a dictionary if necessary. An **X**
indicates that you do not need to put a form in that box.

	NOUN	VERB	ADJECTIVE	ADVERB
1.	assertiveness		assertive	
2.		dominate		X
3.	exception	X		
4.			excessive	
5.		X	inferior	X
6.	myth	X		X
7.	profanity	X		X
8.	proverb	X		X
9.	sexism	X		X
10.	synonym	X		X
11.			talkative	X
12.	uniqueness	X		
13.			valued	X

2 Match the words on the left with their antonyms (opposites) on the right. Use a dictionary if necessary.

_g_ 1. assertiveness   **a.** lack

____ 2. domination   **b.** disregard

____ 3. excess   **c.** submission

____ 4. inferiority   **d.** silence

____ 5. mythical   **e.** common

____ 6. profane   **f.** real

____ 7. talkativeness   ~~**g.** timidity~~

____ 8. unique   **h.** superiority

____ 9. value   **i.** polite

CREATE

Write a paragraph describing the language use of your friends or family members. Use six new words from this unit.

GO TO MyEnglishLab *FOR MORE VOCABULARY PRACTICE.*

GRAMMAR

1 Read the conversation between two male friends. How are the boldfaced phrases similar in meaning? How are they different?

ANTONIO: Where's your wife today?

MINH: She's in her English class.

ANTONIO: Doesn't she know a lot of English?

MINH: She does, but she always wants to learn more. I get bored with English. I can't study languages **as patiently as** she can.

ANTONIO: My wife is the opposite. She hates learning English.

MINH: Not as much as I do. No one learns English **as slowly as** I do!

ANTONIO: That's not true. You've learned it **more quickly than** anyone I know.

COMPARATIVE ADVERBS

Comparative adverbs are used to compare the actions expressed by verbs.	My mother learns English **as quickly as** my father. *(equal)*
	My sister **doesn't** learn English **as quickly as** my brother. *(not equal)*
Actions can be compared by using *as . . . as, not as . . . as, more . . . than,* and *less . . . than.*	Some people study languages **more carefully than** others. *(different)*
	Your teacher explains grammar **less patiently than** mine. *(different)*

2 Complete the paragraph with the comparative form of the adverbs in parentheses.

My sister went to Mexico to learn Spanish. At first, she couldn't speak _____

1. (fluently)

native speakers. Native speakers spoke much _____ she did, so it was difficult

2. (rapidly)

for her to understand them. She spoke a lot _____ they did, and sometimes she

3. (slowly)

had to repeat herself. Her goal was to speak Spanish _____ native speakers, so

4. (skillfully)

she decided to go to language school. There she studied Spanish _____ any other

5. (carefully)

student, so her teacher was very proud of her. After two years of studying Spanish and living in

Mexico, she spoke just a little _____ a native speaker.

6. (perfectly)

3 Think about the last time you spoke English or another foreign language. How did you speak? How did others react to your speaking? On a separate piece of paper, write four sentences. Use a comparative adverb in each.

GO TO MyEnglishLab *TO CHECK WHAT YOU LEARNED.*

FINAL WRITING TASK

In this unit, you read about the way men and women use language to communicate and how this relates to power.

Now you are going to *write a contrast paragraph focusing on two or three important differences between male and female speech in your home culture*. Be sure to use examples to support each difference. Use the vocabulary and grammar from the unit.*

PREPARE TO WRITE: Chart

Use the chart to list some of the ways that males and females use language differently in your home culture. You may consider such differences as topics, gossip, requests and jokes.

	DIFFERENCE 1	DIFFERENCE 2	DIFFERENCE 3	DIFFERENCE 4	DIFFERENCE 5
MALES	Use more impolite words				
FEMALES	Avoid using impolite words				

WRITE: A Contrast Paragraph

When **contrasting**, you explain how two or more ideas are **different**. You can use **point-by-point organization**. When you use point-by-point organization, the points (ideas) in a paragraph are discussed one-by-one.

---

* For Alternative Writing Topics, see page 98. These topics can be used in place of the writing topic for this unit or as homework. The alternative topics relate to the theme of the unit but may not target the same grammar or rhetorical structures taught in the unit.

1 Read the paragraph and look at the point-by-point outline on the next page. Complete the outline with details and examples from the paragraph.

When I speak English, the way I speak is different depending on the situation. One important difference is the formality of language. In class, I can use more informal language because we are all friends. On the other hand, outside of class I don't want to be impolite by speaking too informally. For example, when I'm talking to a clerk in the supermarket, I say, "Would you mind putting that in a bag?" This is more polite than saying, "Put that in a bag." Another difference is asking for help. If I know a person well, I feel comfortable asking what a word means or whether I am saying something correctly. However, if I am speaking to a stranger, I don't like asking for help with my English. Sometimes I pretend to understand something that I don't really understand at all! Finally, I notice that my ability to speak English well depends on the topic. If we discuss a topic in class, I learn a lot of new vocabulary words, and I can express my ideas more easily. On the other hand, sometimes I have trouble with new topics because I don't know enough words in English. These are some of the differences in the ways that I use English, my second language.

Point-by-Point Outline

Point 1: Formality of language

    Details/Examples:

    A. In English class: _____

    B. In the supermarket: _____

Point 2: Asking for help

    Details/Examples:

    A. Speaking to people the writer knows well: _____

    _____

    B. Speaking to strangers: _____

    _____

Point 3: Topics

    Details/Examples:

    A. Topics discussed in class: _____

    _____

    B. Other topics: _____

    _____

2 Use your notes from Prepare to Write, page 93, to write the first draft of your paragraph.

REVISE: Using Transitions of Contrast

1 Read a paragraph about the differences in the male and female use of language. Look at the boldfaced words. What do they mean? Discuss with a partner.

Men and women sometimes have difficulties in their communication with each other. According to linguistic research, a man might get angry when his wife wants to ask a stranger for directions to a park or a restaurant. **Unlike** his wife, he would rather use a map or GPS and find his way by himself. Another language difference is reflected in friendship. For most North American men, talking is not an important part of spending time with a friend. American women, **on the other hand**, usually identify their friends as people with whom they talk frequently. These differences sometimes make it difficult for men and women to communicate. **However**, they can learn to understand their differences and have better relationships.

Writers use **transitions** to help readers move from one idea to another. Transitions help readers understand the relationship between ideas. A variety of transitions are used to show **contrast** (differences) between ideas.

2 Read the information in the box and then complete the exercise that follows.

TRANSITIONS OF CONTRAST

Some transitions of contrast appear at the beginning of a sentence followed by a comma. They can also be placed between the subject and the verb of a sentence.

These include *however* and *on the other hand*.

- Men rarely ask others for directions. **However,** women ask for directions more frequently.
- American women, **on the other hand,** usually identify their friends as people with whom they talk frequently.

Other transitions that begin a sentence are followed by a noun or noun phrase and a comma.

These include *unlike* and *in contrast to*.

- **Unlike** his wife, he would rather use a map or GPS and find his way by himself.
- **In contrast to** women, most American men would rather do things with their friends than talk with them.

Look at the paragraph on page 94. Underline the transitions of contrast.

3 Rewrite the sentences. Use the transition words in parentheses. You may need to change or omit some parts of the sentences.

1. My brother enjoys playing soccer with his friends. My sister would rather spend time talking with hers. (on the other hand)

   _____

2. The English language has developed as part of a culture. Esperanto was developed without any specific culture. (unlike)

   _____

3. Boys often use "report" talk to show their knowledge. Girls often use "rapport" talk to build relationships. (in contrast to)

   _____

4. Men usually want to use a map or GPS to find directions. Women usually want to ask strangers for directions. (on the other hand)

   _____

5. My English class is very informal. The office where I work is very formal. (however)

_____

6. Speaking English to people I know well is easy. Speaking English to strangers is sometimes difficult. (in contrast to)

_____

4 Now go back to the first draft of your paragraph. Where can you add transitions to show the contrast between ideas? Make sure you use the correct transitions and punctuation.

GO TO MyEnglishLab FOR MORE SKILL PRACTICE.

EDIT: Writing the Final Draft

Go to MyEnglishLab and write the final draft of your paragraph. Carefully edit it for grammatical and mechanical errors, such as spelling, capitalization, and punctuation. Make sure you use some of the vocabulary and grammar from the unit. Use the checklist to help you write your final draft. Then submit your paragraph to your teacher.

FINAL DRAFT CHECKLIST

❑ Does your paragraph contain a clear topic sentence stating the main idea?

❑ Does it contain two or three important differences?

❑ Are the differences supported by examples and/or details?

❑ Are transitions of contrast used correctly?

❑ Are commas used to punctuate transitions?

❑ Does your paragraph end with a clear concluding sentence?

❑ Does your paragraph include comparative adverbs?

❑ Does it include new vocabulary from the unit?

UNIT PROJECT

Work in a small group. Research a language that is widely used around the world. Compare your findings and write a report. Follow these steps:

STEP 1: Choose one of these languages:

- Chinese (Mandarin or Cantonese)
- Spanish
- Portuguese
- Arabic
- *your choice*

STEP 2: Use an online encyclopedia or other website to learn about the use of this language today. Answer these questions.

- How widely has this language spread? Where is it spoken?
- Why has this language spread around the world? Consider such factors as trade, exploration, religion, and immigration.
- What other languages, including English, are spoken in areas where this language has spread?
- At what age do students begin learning this language?
- How many non-native speakers does this language have?

STEP 3: Work in a small group to compare your findings. Prepare a report (one paragraph) for the class.

ALTERNATIVE WRITING TOPICS

Write about one of the topics. Use the vocabulary and grammar from the unit.

1. Which languages are spoken in your home culture? Is it important to know English in addition to other languages? Which language is connected with social and economic power? Write a paragraph describing the various languages that are important to people in your home culture.

2. In this unit you learned about English as a global language. Do you think English is helping people around the world to communicate better? Write a paragraph describing a situation in which using English made your communication easier or more difficult. This could be a situation involving school, work, business, shopping, or travel.

3. In many countries today, women are gaining social and economic power. Is this true in your home culture? Consider the lives of women today compared with the lives of women 50 years ago. Are more women becoming educated? Are more women able to earn a living on their own? Write a paragraph to explain.

GO TO MyEnglishLab TO WRITE ABOUT ONE OF THE ALTERNATIVE TOPICS, WATCH A VIDEO ABOUT GENDER AND COMMUNICATION, AND TAKE THE UNIT 4 ACHIEVEMENT TEST.

CAREERS OF THE Future

1. Where is the woman in the photo? What is she doing?

2. What is a career? What is a job? How are they different?

3. What career are you interested in?

READING ONE MEET THE NEW BOSS: YOU

VOCABULARY

1 Read the online advice column from a business newspaper. Pay attention to the boldfaced words.

Ask Danny: Advice for people wanting to work

DEAR DANNY: My job as a film developer is becoming **obsolete** now that everyone takes digital pictures. Can you advise me on how to become a **freelancer** in photography? I think I'm ready to work for myself.—FUTURE FREELANCER

DEAR FUTURE FREELANCER: First of all, becoming a freelancer does not mean that you can stay in your pajamas all day and work when you want. As a freelancer, you have to do everything—get the work, do the work, and collect pay for the work. It's very hard! But here are some basic **strategies** to follow if you are determined to try:

1. Create a website with a blog and be sure to add at least one new photo and some comments about it every day.
2. Decide what types of companies have the photography jobs you want and contact the most likely person to hire photographers at those companies. Don't be afraid to make the first contact. People can't hire you if they don't know about you.
3. Respond to emails and phone calls quickly.
4. Take every job that is offered—even the ones that scare you.

In order to keep a freelance career **sustainable**, you have to work hard for a very long time. And it doesn't offer the job **security** you'd have working for a company, but you will be doing something you love.

DEAR DANNY: I found out today that my job will be **outsourced** next year. The **prospects** for getting another job at my age are few. My hobby is growing flowers, and I'd like to start my own shop with the money I've saved over the years.—FUTURE FLORIST

DEAR FUTURE FLORIST: Using your own money to start a shop is very uncertain. Even the most experienced **entrepreneurs** do not put all their money into one business. So my first piece of advice is to find some partners to share the risk. Then ask yourself these questions:

1. Are you certain you could be an **expert** in growing and arranging flowers professionally?
2. Do you have a location in mind?
3. Have you found a supplier?
4. Do you have the necessary licenses and insurance policies?
5. Do you have a plan to advertise your new shop?

When you can answer "yes" to these questions, you can begin.

2 Circle the correct synonym for each boldfaced word.

1. People who work for the post office are worried that their jobs may become **obsolete**. It's so easy to connect with others online that people don't need to send letters through the mail anymore.

   a. recent   **b.** unnecessary

2. **Freelancers** work for themselves, doing projects for different companies.

   a. independent workers   **b.** retired workers ·

3. College graduates need a **strategy** for finding a career. They need to prepare for their working lives.

   a. resume   **b.** plan

4. Workers can work 15-hour days for a week or two, but working longer is not **sustainable** if product quality is to remain high.

   a. likely to continue   **b.** tiring

5. In Japan the **security** of having the same job for your whole life used to be quite usual. Workers never worried about losing their jobs.

   a. protection from change   **b.** wanting change

6. Companies **outsource** the production of goods as well as service jobs. For example, my brother lost his job making tires when his company moved jobs to Bangladesh.

   a. move workers to another place   **b.** move jobs to another place

(continued on next page)

7. In the next 20 years, there will be an increased need for people to care for greater numbers of aging seniors. So, the **prospects** for careers in the health care field are good.

   a. possibilities   **b.** predictions

8. To be a successful **entrepreneur**, you must be willing to take a risk with your money and your future. You must believe in your ability to grow a profitable company.

   a. person with a new idea   **b.** person with a job

9. **Experts** in computer programming are always needed because they are so talented in writing and developing computer programs

   a. knowledgeable people   **b.** unaware people

GO TO MyEnglishLab FOR MORE VOCABULARY PRACTICE.

PREVIEW

You are going to read a blog about today's new careers. Before you read, look at the list of possible topics. Check (✓) the four topics that you think you will read about.

_____ **1.** How to find the perfect employer

_____ **2.** What kind of job to look for after college

_____ **3.** How to become an entrepreneur

_____ **4.** How to adapt to the new job market

_____ **5.** What to do when you lose your job

_____ **6.** How to find a job with security

Now read the blog on the next page about today's careers.

MEET THE NEW BOSS: YOU

1 People used to be born into a family business or a family career. You'd follow your dad into the sea, the farm, or the workshop. You'd follow your mom into the kitchen or sewing room. In your grandparents' time, there was the **prospect** of working a job from graduation until retirement. How times have changed! Most of my friends have no intention of following in their parents' footsteps[1] or even staying in one job for very long. Working at one particular job for the rest of your life just isn't **sustainable**.

2 In fact, planning to work in the same field or industry for your entire working life just isn't practical anymore. One reason for this is technology. Skills you learn today will be **obsolete** very soon. And then what will you do? Work hard? Win the lottery? Hope for the best or pray? You might be lucky. These **strategies** might bring you a nice, comfy life, working at a job you like and retiring while you're still young and healthy enough to enjoy it. But most of us working today have to look beyond the little box of "career." This means thinking of new ways to make our own money and constantly learning to stay on top of this technology we love and hate and use for everything.

3 If you think you can work eight hours a day and build a career, think again. If you think you can't be replaced by software or have your job **outsourced** to the moon, you are wrong. An employer can always replace you or find someone who can do your job more cheaply. One way to protect yourself is to take what you do at the office and do it on your own as a **freelancer** for a limited time without a contract. For example, if you spend your day editing advertising copy all day, you are developing (and getting good at) a skill that other people want. Editing is a skill that most companies need some of the time. These companies may not offer full-time employment, but they have 100 hours of work that needs to be done now. You step in, get the job done, and get some extra money. You may even find that you make more money as a freelancer and are able to quit your full-time job (*before* it is outsourced).

4 Another strategy is to find something to do besides what you're doing and keep finding a smarter way to do it. That could be turning a hobby into a small business or using your skills to create products and services that you can sell. In other words, think like an **entrepreneur**. Find someone who is willing to help you make your idea a reality. You'll need money, organization, workers, and a lot of energy. You'll need to be a risk taker, an innovator, a problem solver, and

---

[1] **follow in somebody's footsteps:** to do the same job that someone else did before you

(continued on next page)

a hard worker. Being an entrepreneur is not an 8-hour-a-day job; it is a 24-hour-a-day job. And when things go well, you have your rewards. Here's an example. A woman I grew up with decided to become a chef. Then she developed a wedding cake business. A few years later, she started blogging about desserts and writing restaurant reviews for a website. One thing leads to another, especially if you can become an **expert** at something.

5   Jobs and careers come and go at an amazing pace these days. What if your job disappears after working for 10 years in the field? You may have to go back to school to be able to work in another field. You may have to retrain yourself in order to keep working at the same company or in the same field. In fact, in all likelihood, you will have to do this more than once.

6   In short, if you are going to succeed in the twenty-first-century job market, you have to broaden your idea of what earning a living is. Lifetime **security** from one employer is no longer certain or even likely. The truth is that you will probably have several jobs in different fields in your lifetime; you may even work as a freelancer or form your own company. Are you ready for this new type of career?

MAIN IDEAS

1   Look again at the Preview on page 104. How did your predictions help you understand the blog?

2   Read the statements. They all give bad career advice. Rewrite each one to make it reflect one of the main ideas of the reading.

1. If you find the right job, you can work there for your entire career.

_____

2. Most employers offer job security to their employees.

_____

3. If you lose your job and can't find a new one, you can easily become an entrepreneur.

_____

4. Becoming an expert in one job is enough to support you.

_____

DETAILS

To paraphrase a sentence means to say it in a different way, using your own words. The sentences below are paraphrases of sentences in the blog. Write the exact sentence from the blog that has the same meaning as the paraphrase. Refer to the paragraph in parentheses.

1. Years ago, you could start working in one place and work there all your life. *(paragraph 1)*

   In your grandparents' time, there was the prospect of working a job from _graduation until retirement._

2. The abilities you have today won't be needed in the future. *(paragraph 2)*

3. Most workers have to think of more than just one type of job. *(paragraph 2)*

4. Your boss could hire someone to do your job for less money. *(paragraph 3)*

5. Develop an independent skill and try to do it differently and better than others. *(paragraph 4)*

6. You'll need a partner who wants you to succeed. *(paragraph 4)*

7. Taking chances, being creative, thinking of solutions, and being tireless are what you need. *(paragraph 4)*

MAKE INFERENCES

RECOGNIZING IRONY

An **inference** is an **educated guess** about something that is **not directly stated** in a text. Writers sometimes use **irony** in this way. Is the writer being serious? Or is the writer being sarcastic, exaggerating, joking, or even saying the opposite of what he or she means?

Is the idea something that you would expect to read, or is it surprising?

Look at the example and read the explanation.

• "And then what will you do? Work hard? Win the lottery? Hope for the best or pray?"

In this text, the author offers suggestions of what to do if your job becomes obsolete, but none of these strategies is realistic:

Work hard? Here the author is being **sarcastic**; you might be a very hard worker, but it's hard to work hard when your job is gone.

Win the lottery? Here the author is **exaggerating** because very few people win the lottery.

Hope for the best or pray? And here, he is being **humorous**. Everyone knows that getting a new job requires more than hoping and praying.

After reading the text closely, we can **recognize** that the author is using **irony** (sarcasm, exaggeration, and humor), and we can **infer** that he is **not being serious** and **wants to surprise** the reader.

Check (✓) the phrases and sentences from the reading that show irony. Then discuss your answers with a classmate. Refer to the paragraphs in parentheses. Explain the examples of irony.

_____ **1.** Skills you learn today will be obsolete very soon. *(paragraph 2)*

___✓___ **2.** You might be lucky. These strategies might bring you a nice, comfy life. *(paragraph 2)*

_____ **3.** Look beyond the little box of "career." *(paragraph 2)*

_____ **4.** This means constantly learning to stay on top of this technology. *(paragraph 2)*

_____ **5.** If you think you can work eight hours a day and build a career, think again. *(paragraph 3)*

_____ **6.** If you think you can't be replaced by software or have your job outsourced to the moon, you are wrong. *(paragraph 3)*

_____ **7.** You are developing (and getting good at) a skill that other people want. *(paragraph 3)*

_____ **8.** Quit your job (before it is outsourced). *(paragraph 3)*

_____ **9.** Find someone who is willing to help you make your idea a reality. *(paragraph 4)*

_____ **10.** Being an entrepreneur is not an 8-hour-a-day job; it is a 24-hour-a-day job. *(paragraph 4)*

EXPRESS OPINIONS

Work in groups of three. Choose one of the questions below. Discuss your ideas. Then choose one person in your group to report the ideas to the class.

1. In your experience, do people no longer follow in their parents' career footsteps? Would you follow your parents' career?

2. Do you agree with the author's ideas about freelancing? Would you consider being a freelancer in order to find more work?

3. Which jobs are more likely / less likely to be outsourced in coming years? Why?

■■■■■■■■■■■■■■■■■■■■■■■■■■■■■ *GO TO* MyEnglishLab *TO GIVE YOUR OPINION ABOUT ANOTHER QUESTION.*

READING TWO | GREAT JOBS FOR THE TWENTY-FIRST CENTURY

READ

1 Look at the boldfaced words in the reading on the next page and think about the questions.

1. Which words do you know the meaning of?

2. Can you use any of the words in a sentence?

2 Now read the information from an online career center brochure about jobs for the twenty-first century.

Great Jobs for the Twenty-first Century

Social Media Managers

1   At the start of the twenty-first century, there was no Facebook or Twitter. But companies today have to plan strategies for using social media to communicate with customers. They are seeking experts who understand the **benefits** of staying in touch.

Game Designers and Developers

2   With the huge popularity of online games, this career attracts many and is not limited to entertainment. Improving technology can also be used in training, education, and therapy. Jobs in this field are available to artists as well as to experts in artificial intelligence.

Cybersecurity Officers

3   The role of a cybersecurity officer is to **ensure** the safety and privacy of personal information collected by institutions such as universities and banks. Both business and tech majors will enjoy making sure that hackers[1] and thieves are stopped by finding out their methods.

Health Care Professionals

4   As more dentists retire, there will not be enough new dentists to replace them. And that means there will be many job opportunities for dental assistants to help with the extra work. There will also be a high demand for doctors and nurses.

Biomedical Engineers

5   As the science of biotechnology develops, more biomedical engineers will be needed. People are living longer, and this is partly due to biomedical engineering. A biomedical engineer applies the principles and design of engineering to medicine. The results so far have been in the fields of genetic engineering and brain mapping.

Physical and Occupational Therapists

6   When people break a bone or are **injured**, their lives are upset in many ways. Physical therapists can help heal the physical injury, and occupational therapists can train the patient to live a normal life again. These are jobs that will always be necessary.

---

[1] **hackers:** people who secretly use or change the information in other people's computer systems

Sustainability Directors

7   The goal of sustainability is to make sure that natural resources such as land and water will be available to future generations.[2] As companies become more concerned about the natural environment, they will look to sustainability directors to help them reduce waste[3] and pollution by finding more earth-friendly ways of producing and selling goods.

Asteroid Mining Engineers

8   In the twenty-first century, new technologies will be used to explore space and to find important resources, including metals and water. Asteroids, the small rocky planets located between Mars and Jupiter, have both. As entrepreneurs plan the mining of asteroid resources, there will be a need for mining engineers to make decisions and provide direction.

Astrophysicists

9   In the twenty-first century, the exploration of space will become more and more common and important. And in order to explore space, an understanding of the universe and its physical properties is necessary. Astrophysicists study the universe's density, temperature, and chemical makeup and then analyze the data. With more countries—and private companies—investigating the universe, astrophysicists will be in demand.

---

[2] **generations:** all people of about the same age
[3] **waste:** unwanted materials or substances that are left after you have used something

COMPREHENSION

Read the statements and mark them **T** (true) or **F** (false). Rewrite the false statements to make them true.

_____ **1.** Game designers are not limited to developing entertainment.

_____ **2.** Cybersecurity officers only work for businesses.

_____ **3.** The field of biomedical engineering started because people are living longer.

_____ **4.** Sustainability directors help companies be more earth-friendly.

_____ **5.** Astrophysicists are interested in finding water in space.

GO TO MyEnglishLab FOR MORE VOCABULARY PRACTICE.

READING SKILL

1 Look at Reading Two again. How many subheadings does it have?

PREDICTING CONTENT FROM TITLE AND SUBHEADINGS

One way to predict the content of a text is to look at its title and subheadings:

- A good **title** is a brief **summary of the main idea of the whole reading**.
- A good **subheading** is a brief **summary of the content of a section** of the reading.

Look at the title and subheadings of Reading Two and read the explanations.

- The **title** ("Great Jobs for the Twenty-first Century") indicates the main idea of the reading.
- The **subheadings** give you more specific information about that topic: the names of several kinds of jobs. By reading the subheadings, you can find the group of jobs that you are interested in and focus your attention quickly on those.

2 Go back to Reading Two. Read the subheadings quickly. Think about which job category they belong in. Write them in the columns. Compare your answers with another student.

COMPUTERS	MEDICINE	SPACE	ENVIRONMENT
Social media managers			

GO TO MyEnglishLab FOR MORE SKILL PRACTICE.

STEP 1: Organize

Reading One (**R1**) and Reading Two (**R2**) contain information about the careers of the future. Look at the chart listing some of the features mentioned in Reading One and some of the jobs mentioned in Reading Two. Check (✓) the box where the job seems to have that feature, and put an **X** if the job does not. Share your answers with the class.

R1 ⟍ R2	JOB SECURITY	POSSIBILITY OF BEING OUTSOURCED	OPPORTUNITIES FOR ENTREPRENEURS	OPPORTUNITIES FOR FREELANCERS
Social media managers	X	✓	✓	✓
Game designers and developers				
Cybersecurity officers				
Health care professionals				
Biomedical engineers				
Asteroid mining engineers				
Astrophysicists				

STEP 2: Synthesize

Work with a partner to complete the dialogue between two university seniors. They're discussing the pros and cons of different careers. Use information from the chart in Step 1.

CARLOS: Did you go to the job fair today?

NU AHN: Yes. I found it very interesting and informative.

CARLOS: Me, too. I was particularly interested in the jobs in medicine because _they offer job security. No one can outsource a doctor's job!_

(continued on next page)

Careers of the Future   113

Nu Ahn: I liked learning about careers related to space like _____
_____.

Unfortunately, I don't have the time or money to get more education, so I was looking
at _____. I think a job as a game developer
_____._____.

Carlos: I think I'd rather work more directly with people. In medicine, _____
_____.

Plus, in the future, _____._____
_____.

Nu Ahn: I understand, but I'd rather be able to work at home. Maybe _____
_____
_____.

Carlos: I guess we're different. Glad there are so many careers to choose from!

GO TO MyEnglishLab TO CHECK WHAT YOU LEARNED.

VOCABULARY

Read the essay about jobs and careers in the United States during the last century. Complete the essay with words from the box.

benefits	~~experts~~	obsolete	security
ensure	freelancers	outsourced	strategies
entrepreneur	injured	prospects	sustainable

Jobs and Careers in the United States (1900–2000)

Not surprisingly, the job market is changing today as it has done since people started working

for other people. The workforce and working conditions especially changed during the twentieth

century.

In 1900, most workers farmed or produced goods for sale. Employers weren't looking for

_____experts_____ in farming or producing goods. The only job requirements for these jobs
     1.

were a healthy body and a willingness to work hard.

At that time, women were only 19 percent of the total number of workers, and children under

15 were 6 percent of workers. The workweek was 53 hours, and you probably wouldn't keep your

job for more than a year. So the _____ for long-term employment were not good.
                              2.

The working conditions weren't safe, and many accidents happened. Workers were sometimes

_____ on the job. In some industries such as mining or railroad, workers were
          3.

even killed. Wages were comparatively low, and there was no sick pay if you had to miss a day

or more of work. There was no sick pay if you had to miss a day or more of work. There was no

health insurance that would pay your bills if you were hurt on the job. And if you were out too

long, your boss might hire someone else, so the idea of job _____ didn't really
                                       4.

(continued on next page)

exist. Bosses didn't think there were _____ 5. in keeping workers because there were always other people eager to work.

In 1900, no one used the word _____ 6. , but people with a lot money invested in their own ideas or in other people's. As long as they could _____ 7. a profit, they were willing to foot the bill.[1] Women often had to stay at home with their children, but they could earn money by sewing or cooking for others in their homes. They didn't call themselves _____ 8. , but that's what they were.

In the second half of the century, many jobs such as milkman and iceman became _____ 9. . People didn't need to have milk delivered every day, and they had electric refrigerators, so they didn't need ice to keep things cold at home. At the same time, other occupations grew at a quick rate. Later in the century, service industry jobs increased by 47 percent, and because people began to be concerned about developing _____ 10. use of the Earth's resources, jobs that are related to protecting the environment also increased. In the latter part of the century, computers and the Internet became commonplace, and technicians who understood these machines were needed to fix them. The number of entrepreneurs increased by 60 percent, and freelance work became the only means of support for thousands of workers. In fact, it is estimated that by the year 2020, half of the workforce will be freelancers.

As the century closed, jobs were being eliminated or _____ 11. to other countries at an increasing rate. It was becoming clear that workers needed to find new ways to earn money and new _____ 12. for finding jobs. They had to design careers that would support them for their whole lives.

---

[1] **foot the bill:** pay for something

1 Fill in the chart with the adjective form of the given words. Use a dictionary if you need to.

	NOUN/VERBS	ADJECTIVE
1.	benefit	*beneficial*
2.	entrepreneur	
3.	expert	
4.	occupation	
5.	prospect	
6.	strategy	
7.	sustain	

2 Match an adjective on the left with a noun on the right to make up a common idiomatic expression (see its definition in parentheses).

   b   **1. beneficial**   **a. employer** (someone who might hire you)

_____ **2. entrepreneurial**   ~~**b. relationship** (good for two people)~~

_____ **3. expert**   **c. growth** (growth that continues itself)

_____ **4. occupational**   **d. hazard** (an injury that happens when you're working)

_____ **5. prospective**   **e. location** (the best location to be at a certain time)

_____ **6. strategic**   **f. spirit** (full of ideas to make money)

_____ **7. sustainable**   **g. advice** (suggestions from knowledgeable people in a particular field

3 Write the eight expressions you came up with. You will need them for the next activity.

1. _____*beneficial relationship*_____   5. _____

2. _____   6. _____

3. _____   7. _____

4. _____   8. _____

CREATE

Complete this email to a software company from a recent college graduate who is looking for a job. The graduate is writing to the personnel director, who has advertised for several software design jobs.

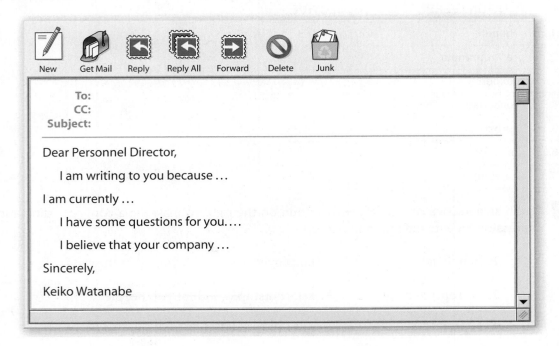

New   Get Mail   Reply   Reply All   Forward   Delete   Junk

To:
CC:
Subject:

Dear Personnel Director,

   I am writing to you because ...

I am currently ...

   I have some questions for you. ...

   I believe that your company ...

Sincerely,

Keiko Watanabe

GO TO MyEnglishLab FOR MORE VOCABULARY PRACTICE.

GRAMMAR

1 Read these sentences. Look at the boldfaced verbs. What is the difference between the verb forms? Notice the words in italics. What do they indicate?

- *As* more dentists **retire**, there **will not be** enough new dentists to replace them.
- *When* entrepreneurs **plan** the mining of asteroid resources, they **will need** mining engineers to make decisions and provide direction.
- *Before* the company **hires** you, they **will do** a security check of your background.

FUTURE TIME CLAUSES

1. **Future time clauses** show the time relationship between **two future events**:

   - the verb in the **main clause** is in the **future** tense *(will be* or *going to)*
   - the verb in the **time clause** is in the **present** tense

   Be Careful! Do NOT use *will* or *be going to* in the time clause.

   The **time clause** starts with a **time expression** like *before* or *when*. It comes at the beginning or at the end of the sentence.

   Main Clause
   They **will check** your background
   Time Clause
   before they **hire** you.

   NOT before they ~~will~~ hire you

   Time Clause   Main Clause
   When things **go** well, you **will be** rewarded.

   NOT: when things ~~will~~ go well

2. When the **time clause** comes at the **beginning** of the sentence, put a **comma** after the time clause.

   Do NOT use a comma if it comes at the end.

   After the new company opens, many people will apply for jobs.

   I will apply *when* the jobs are posted.

   NOT: I will ~~apply, when~~ the jobs are posted.

3. These common **time expressions** are used to begin time clauses:

   a. *when, as, after, as soon as* (to introduce the event that happened first)

   b. *before, until, by the time* (to introduce the event that happens second)

   c. *while* (to introduce an event that will happen at the same time as another event)

   As soon as my report is finished, I'm going to go home.

   By the time the sun comes up tomorrow, I will be finished with my report.

   While I am writing, I will use spell check.

---

2 Complete the conversation with the correct form of the verbs in parentheses. Notice that some sentences are questions.

TINA: Are you ready for your job interview tomorrow?

SUE: I'm not sure. What happens at a job interview? I've never had one.

TINA: Really? Here's what will probably happen. As soon as you _____*enter*_____, people
1. (enter)
_____*will look*_____ at you. Be professional, and dress well. While you are waiting, you
2. (look)
may get nervous. Try to relax. Take a deep breath.

SUE: OK. When I _____ nervous, I _____ a deep breath.
3. (be)   4. (take)

(continued on next page)

TINA: Right. The first question the interviewers will ask will probably be general. They will ask you to describe yourself and your experience. Also, interviewers always ask about your strengths and weaknesses. So, what _____ when the interviewer

5. (you/say)

_____ you about these? Have you thought about this?

6. (ask)

SUE: No! But I _____ it before I _____ tomorrow.

7. (think)　　　　　　　　8. (go)

TINA: The interviewers will ask you why you want the job. They will also want to know what you know about their company.

SUE: Oh no! When I _____ that answer, what _____?

9. (know/not)　　　　　　10. (the interviewers/do)

TINA: Nothing, but you probably won't make a good impression.

SUE: OK. Before I _____ on the interview, I _____ about the

11. (go)　　　　　　　　12. (learn)

company. I'm going to start studying and thinking right now.

TINA: Good idea.

3 Combine the two sentences by using the time expression in parentheses. Pay attention to comma use.

1. (before)
   - The year will end.
   - Ten percent of the employees will lose their jobs.

     Before the year ends, 10 percent of the employees will lose their jobs. OR
     Ten percent of the employees will lose their jobs before the year ends.

2. (when)
   - The new boss will arrive.
   - We will be on our best behavior.

   _____

3. (as soon as)
   - The boss will interview prospective employees.
   - The boss will have time.

   _____

4. (while)

- We will be in the office.
- We will check the numbers.

_____

5. (after)

- The office party will end.
- Who will clean up?

_____

6. (when)

- We will drive to work.
- We will pick up your friend.

_____

7. (as)

- Opportunities will arise.
- People will take advantage of them.

_____

8. (as soon as)

- Our business will make enough money.
- We will open another store.

_____

GO TO MyEnglishLab _TO CHECK WHAT YOU LEARNED._

FINAL WRITING TASK

In this unit, you read about what careers will be like in the future and also about some examples of those careers

Now you are going to *write a cover letter for a prospective employer*. The job you will apply for is your ideal job. Use the vocabulary and grammar from the unit.*

PREPARE TO WRITE: Freewriting

Freewriting is a **technique that writers use to help them gather ideas**. When you use this technique, you write **as much as you can about the topic** you will discuss in your paragraph or essay. You shouldn't worry about word choice, grammar, spelling, or punctuation. No one will see your freewriting paper except you. You just keep writing. When you are finished, you can choose ideas and then expand on them.

Freewrite for 10 minutes about your ideal job. Don't evaluate; just write.

WRITE: A Cover Letter

STRUCTURING A COVER LETTER

A cover letter has three parts: an **introduction, supporting points,** and a **conclusion.** The specific content for each part is particular to the job you are applying for, but the basic content is the same for all cover letters.

Introductory paragraph

In this paragraph, you should introduce yourself and express interest in a specific position in the company. Be clear in your purpose for writing, and be brief.

Supporting paragraph(s)

In this paragraph, you need to focus on your experience and how it will meet the needs of the company. If you can, give specific examples of how you have completed projects and solved problems. Do not write more than two paragraphs. Since employers have to read many cover letters, being brief is important.

Concluding paragraph

This paragraph should sum up your interest in the position. Include a reference to the résumé that you have enclosed and your availability for an interview. Be sure to thank the employer for reading your letter with a phrase like "Thank you for your attention."

---

* For Alternative Writing Topics, see page 127. These topics can be used in place of the writing topic for this unit or as homework. The alternative topics relate to the theme of the unit but may not target the same grammar or rhetorical structures taught in the unit

1 Read the cover letter and answer the questions.

1. Identify the three parts of a cover letter.

2. Does each part contain appropriate content?

Chris Young
47 E. Tempe Road
Tempe, AZ 85281
602-123-4567
chris@xyz.com

January 2, 2014

Thomas L. Jones
Personnel Director
Planetary Resources
350 S. Madison Ave.
Bellevue, WA 98004
tlj@planetaryresources.org

Dear Mr. Jones,

I am writing to apply because the job title "General Space Nut" seemed to be the kind of job I am looking for. And your company is the type of place I'm looking for to begin my career. I believe I have the qualifications that you're looking for and would be interested in knowing more about your organization.

I recently graduated with a doctorate in geology and mining from the University of Arizona's department of planetary sciences. However, since it seems you are more interested in a candidate's personality than his education, let me tell you a little bit about myself: I was the adolescent who was out exploring the desert instead of doing homework, and I was (still am) crazy about rocks. As a graduate student, I led field trips to deserts in Arizona and California to study the rock formations. Adding the study of asteroids to the study of earth geology would be an incredibly exciting challenge for me, and I am ready to throw all my energy into it. I believe that asteroid mining is the way of the future, and I want to devote my career to it.

In short, I am eager to learn more about Planetary Resources and how I can fit into the organization. I am a person who would add to the successes you have and figure out the failures. I have enclosed a résumé with more details about me, and I am available to meet with you at your convenience. Thank you for your attention.

Sincerely,

Chris Young

Chris Young

2 Look at the freewriting exercise you did in the Prepare to Write section, page 122. Check (✓) the content areas for each paragraph, and make notes about each from your freewriting. Add information for those areas you didn't freewrite about or where you don't have enough detail.

Introductory Paragraph:

❏ introduce self _____

❏ identify job _____

❏ state purpose _____

Supporting Paragraph:

❏ discuss experience _____

❏ relate experience to the position/company _____

❏ describe specific example(s) _____

Concluding Paragraph:

❏ summarize your interest _____

❏ refer to enclosed résumé _____

❏ indicate availability for interview _____

❏ thank the employer _____

3 Write the first draft of your letter. It should have three paragraphs. Use the letter format in the sample.

REVISE: Using the Correct Letter Format

1 You can send your cover letter by email in an attachment, or you can mail it. In either case, you need to be sure that you have the correct format.

COVER LETTER FORMAT

The five parts of a cover letter format are **your address, the date, the inside address, the greeting,** and **the closing**.

- **Your address** should be placed on the upper right-hand side of the paper or document. Include your email address after the phone number.

- Leave one space and put **the date**.

- Leave one space, and put **the inside address** at the left-hand margin. The inside address is the name, position, address, phone number, and email address of the person you are writing to.

- **The greeting** (also called the **salutation**) is the opening to the letter.
  - If you know the name of the person, write
    Dear Mr. Smith,
    Dear Ms. Smith,

  - If you are not sure whether the person is a man or a woman, write the full name.
    Dear Chris Young,

  - If you don't have the name of a specific person, you can write the title of the position.
    Dear Personnel Director,

  - If you don't have any information, you can write a generic greeting.
    To whom it may concern,

- **The closing** is a short phrase followed by your signature.

    Sincerely,

    Respectfully yours,

2 Write the parts of the letter format in the correct place.

a. closing

b. inside address

c. your address

d. greeting

e. date

_____

_____

_____

_____

Xxxxxxxxxxxxxxxxxxxxxxxxxxxx
xxxxxxxxxxxxxxxxxxxxxxxxxxxxxxxx
xxxxxx.
    Xxxxxxxxxxxxxxxxxxxxxxxxxxx
xxxxxxxxxxxxxxxxxxxxxxxxxxxxxxxx
xxxxxx.
    Xxxxxxxxxxxxxxxxxxxxxxxxxx
xxxxxxxxxxxxxxxxxxxxxxxxxxxxxxx
xxxxxx.

_____

3 Now go back to the first draft of your cover letter. Does it have the correct cover letter format? If not, please revise.

GO TO MyEnglishLab FOR MORE SKILL PRACTICE.

EDIT: Writing the Final Draft

Go to MyEnglishLab and write the final draft of your cover letter with good cover letter format. Carefully edit it for grammatical and mechanical errors, such as spelling, capitalization, and punctuation. Make sure that you use some of the vocabulary and grammar from the unit. Use the checklist to help you write your final draft. Then submit your cover letter to your teacher.

FINAL DRAFT CHECKLIST

❏ Does your cover letter contain a brief introductory paragraph that clearly explains why you're writing?

❏ Does the introductory paragraph include the name of the position?

❏ Does the supporting paragraph focus on how your skills would meet the employer's needs?

❏ Does the supporting paragraph contain one or two specific examples?

❏ Does the concluding paragraph summarize why you want the job? Does it thank the employer?

❏ Does your letter have correct cover letter format?

❏ Are there future time clauses with verbs in the correct tense?

❏ Do these clauses have the correct punctuation?

❏ Do you use new vocabulary from the unit?

UNIT PROJECT

Work with your class. Make posters about different types of jobs that are available in your area. Then organize a job fair where you tell your classmates about one type of job and you learn about other types of jobs. Follow these steps:

STEP 1: To begin, your teacher and your class will brainstorm types of local jobs. Are there big companies in your area? Is there a particular industry? For example, Seattle, Washington, has a lot of computer companies. Then you and one partner will work closely to research one kind of job.

STEP 2: Go online and research the type of job that you chose in Step I. You can start with one of these job–searching websites. On each of them you enter the type of job and the location.

- craigslist
- Simply Hired
- Career Builder
- Indeed

STEP 3: Choose one job and make a poster about the position available so you can display it at the job fair. On the poster, you should include:

- the name and description of the job
- the company and its location
- the qualifications and skills needed for the position
- the wages or salary

STEP 4: On the day of the job fair, you and your partner will choose a place in the classroom and create a table which has information about your job. Take turns with your partner sitting at the table and talking to your classmates who are visiting the tables. While you are at the table, your partner can go around the classroom and learn about other jobs.

ALTERNATIVE WRITING TOPICS

Write about one of the topics. Use the vocabulary and grammar from the unit.

1. Write a paragraph describing another career that you think will be common in the future. Give reasons to explain why this type of job will be important.

2. In this unit, you read about the advantages of working for yourself and not for an employer. What do you think are the disadvantages of working for yourself? Would you prefer to work for yourself or for an employer? Write a paragraph to explain.

3. In this unit, you read about family occupations or work that members of a family have done for generations. Write a paragraph describing an occupation that members of your family have shared. Do you plan to continue this occupation? Why or why not?

GO TO MyEnglishLab *TO WRITE ABOUT ONE OF THE ALTERNATIVE TOPICS, WATCH A VIDEO ABOUT CAREERS, AND TAKE THE UNIT 5 ACHIEVEMENT TEST.*

WHAT IS
Ecotourism?

1 FOCUS ON THE TOPIC

1. More and more people are traveling to Antarctica. Why do you think they want to go there?

2. What is *ecotourism*? What do ecology[1] and tourism have in common?

3. Describe a place that you have visited that had lots of natural beauty (trees, mountains, an ocean, and so on). Have visitors damaged or harmed this place in any way?

---

[1] **ecology:** the way in which plants, animals, and people are related to each other and to their environment, or the study of this

GO TO MyEnglishLab *TO CHECK WHAT YOU KNOW.*

VOCABULARY

1 Study the words and definitions.

1. **coastal:** in the ocean or on the land near the shore (the area where the land meets the water)

2. **consequence:** something that happens as a result of a particular action or situation

3. **fragile:** easily broken, damaged, or ruined

4. **harsh:** difficult to live in and very uncomfortable

5. **inhabit:** to live in an area or a place

6. **landscape:** the way an area of land looks

7. **preserve:** to save something or someone from being harmed or destroyed

8. **remote:** far away from towns and cities

9. **research:** serious study of a subject, especially in order to discover new facts or test new ideas

10. **tourist:** someone who is traveling or visiting a place for pleasure

11. **vast:** extremely large

2 How much do you know about Antarctica? Take this quiz—just for fun. Circle the answer you think best. Pay special attention to the boldfaced words.

1. About _____ of Antarctica's **vast** land is covered with ice.

    a. 25%   **c.** 75%

    b. 50%   **d.** 98%

2. While Antarctica's **landscape** appears cold and snowy, the land of Antarctica is actually a _____.

    a. desert   **c.** jungle

    b. forest   **d.** plain

3. The coldest temperature of the **harsh** Antarctic winter is approximately _____.

    a. −35°C   **c.** −90°C

    b. −50°C   **d.** −120°C

4. Antarctica is **inhabited** by penguins and other animals, including _____.

   a. bears   **c.** eagles

   b. seals   **d.** snow leopards

5. In _____, a group of explorers led by Roald Amundsen became the first people to reach the **remote** South Pole.

   a. 1890   **c.** 1920

   b. 1911   **d.** 1952

6. The number of **tourists** visiting Antarctica increased from 4,698 in 1991 to approximately _____ in 2012.

   a. 8,000   **c.** 18,000

   b. 10,000   **d.** 27,000

7. In _____, 12 countries signed the Antarctic Treaty to **preserve** the continent for scientific **research**.

   a. 1959   **c.** 1990

   b. 1978   **d.** 2002

8. In _____, Emilio Palma was the first person born in Antarctica; his parents were living in the **coastal** area of Hope Bay.

   a. 1878   **c.** 1978

   b. 1950   **d.** 2006

9. Antarctica is colder than the Arctic as a **consequence** of its elevation; most of the continent is more than _____ above sea level.

   a. $^1/_2$ kilometer   **c.** 10 kilometers

   b. 2 kilometers   **d.** 50 kilometers

10. In 1999, Tim Jarvis and Peter Treseder walked across the **fragile** Antarctic environment to the South Pole in _____ days.

    a. 25   **c.** 46

    b. 36   **d.** 99

GO TO MyEnglishLab FOR MORE VOCABULARY PRACTICE.

Answer Key: 1. d, 2. a, 3. c, 4. b, 5. b, 6. d, 7. a, 8. c, 9. b, 10. c

PREVIEW

Read the first paragraph of an opinion essay about tourism in Antarctica, written by a scientist who works there. Predict reasons why the scientist says, "I feel Antarctica should be closed to tourists." Write your ideas on the lines. Then share your ideas with the class.

1. _____

2. _____

3. _____

Now read the rest of the essay.

Tourists in a Fragile Land

1   As a scientist working in Antarctica, I spend most of my time in the lab studying ice. I am trying to find out the age of Antarctic ice. All we know for certain is that it is the oldest ice in the world. The more we understand it, the more we will understand the changing weather of the Earth. Today, as with an increasing number of days, I had to leave my work to greet a group of **tourists** who were taking a vacation in this continent of ice. And even though I can appreciate their desire to experience this **vast** and beautiful **landscape**, I feel Antarctica should be closed to tourists.

2   Because Antarctica is the center of important scientific **research**, it must be **preserved** for this purpose. Meteorologists are now looking at the effects of the ozone hole[1] that was discovered above Antarctica in 1984. They are also trying to understand global warming.[2] If the Earth's temperature continues to increase, the health and safety of every living thing on the planet will be affected. Astronomers have a unique view of space and are able to see it very clearly from Antarctica. Biologists have a chance to learn more about the animals that **inhabit** the **coastal** areas of this frozen land. Botanists study the plant life to understand how it can live in such a **harsh** environment, and geologists study the Earth to learn more about how it was formed. There are even psychologists who study how people behave when they live and work together in such a **remote** location.

3   Tourists in Antarctica can damage scientific research and hurt the environment. When tourist groups come here, they take us away from our research. Our work is difficult, and some of our projects can be damaged by such simple mistakes as opening the wrong door or bumping into a small piece of equipment. In addition, tourists in Antarctica can also hurt the environment. Members of Greenpeace, one of the world's leading environmental

---

[1] **ozone hole:** a hole in the layer of gases that protect the Earth from the bad effects of the sun

[2] **global warming:** a general increase in world temperatures caused by increased amounts of carbon dioxide around the Earth

organizations, complain that tourists leave trash on beaches and disturb the plants and animals. In a place as frozen as Antarctica, it can take 100 years for a plant to grow back, and tourists can easily damage penguin eggs. Oil spills are another problem caused by tourism. Oil spills not only kill penguins but can also destroy scientific projects.

4   The need to protect Antarctica from tourists becomes even greater when we consider the fact that there is no government here. Antarctica belongs to no country. Who is making sure that the penguins, plants, and sea are safe? No one is responsible. In fact, we scientists are only temporary visitors ourselves. It is true that the number of tourists who visit Antarctica each year is small compared to the number of those who visit other places. However, these other places are inhabited by local residents and controlled by local governments. They have an interest in protecting their natural environments.

Who is concerned about the environment of Antarctica? The scientists, to be sure, but not necessarily the tour companies that make money from sending people south.

5   If we don't protect Antarctica from tourism, there may be serious **consequences** for us all. We might lose the results of scientific research projects. It's possible that these results could teach us something important about the causes and effects of climate change. Some **fragile** plants and animals might die and disappear forever. This could damage the balance of animal and plant life in Antarctica. We know from past experience that when things get unbalanced, harmful changes can occur. Clearly, Antarctica should remain a place for careful and controlled scientific research. We cannot allow tourism to bring possible danger to the planet. The only way to protect this fragile and important part of the planet is to stop tourists from traveling to Antarctica.

MAIN IDEAS

1 Look again at the Preview on page 132. How did your predictions help you understand the essay?

2 In the body of his essay (paragraphs 2, 3, 4), the scientist gives three main reasons why Antarctica should be closed to tourists. Number the reasons in the order in which they appear in Reading One.

_____ There is no government to protect Antarctica.

_____ Tourists can damage scientific research that can be conducted only in Antarctica.

_____ Tourists can damage Antarctica's environment.

DETAILS

1 Complete the outline with details from Reading One.

> **I.** Scientists learn new things in Antarctica because it is different from other places. Antarctica has:
>
> **A.** _____ ice in the world
>
> **B.** a unique _____ of space
>
> **C.** a very _____ environment
>
> **II.** Problems in Antarctica may have negative effects, such as:
>
> **A.** loss of the results of scientific _____
>
> **B.** disappearance of _____
>
> **C.** damage to the balance of _____

2 These statements are false or incomplete. Rewrite them according to Reading One so that they are true and complete.

1. The author of the essay knows the age of Antarctic ice.

The writer of the essay is trying to find out the age of Antarctic ice.

2. The writer wants Antarctica to be closed.

_____

3. Psychologists study how people behave when they get lost in Antarctica.

_____

4. Oil spills in Antarctica have killed scientists.

_____

5. Tour companies may be concerned about the environment of Antarctica.

_____

6. If we don't protect Antarctica from tourism, there will be serious consequences for a few scientists.

_____

7. We know from past experience that when things get balanced, harmful changes can occur.

MAKE INFERENCES

INFERRING PROBABILITY

An **inference** is an **educated guess** about something that is **not directly stated** in a text. Writers sometimes **suggest whether something is likely or unlikely** without directly stating it.

Look at the example and read the explanation.

- "Because Antarctica is the center for important scientific research, it must be preserved for this purpose." *(paragraph 2)*

We will find out about different types of scientists that work in Antarctica. Choose the best answer.

a. Likely
b. Unlikely
*(The best answer is **a**.)*

In **paragraph 2** the author tells us that Antarctica should be preserved because it is very important for scientific research. Since this is the topic sentence of the paragraph, we can guess that the paragraph will contain more information about different types of scientists working in Antarctica.

After reading the text closely, we can **infer** that it is **likely** that we will find out about different types of scientists that work in Antarctica.

Read the statements. Choose the best answer to indicate how likely or unlikely it is. Refer to the paragraphs in parentheses.

1. Tourists make living in Antarctica stressful. *(paragraph 3)*

   a. likely   **b.** unlikely

2. For Greenpeace, Antarctica is one of the most important areas in the world. *(paragraph 3)*

   a. likely   **b.** unlikely

3. Antarctica will form a government. *(paragraph 4)*

   a. likely   **b.** unlikely

4. Scientists enjoy tourists. *(paragraph 5)*

   a. likely   **b.** unlikely

Now discuss your answers with a partner. Point out in the paragraphs the sentences, words, or phrases that helped you find the answers.

EXPRESS OPINIONS

Work in groups of three. Choose one of the questions. Discuss your ideas. Then choose one person in your group to report the ideas to the class.

1. If you were a scientist in Antarctica, how would you feel about tourists? Explain.

2. Can you find any weaknesses in the writer's opinion? Do you agree with everything he says? How much do you agree with him?

3. Would you be interested in visiting Antarctica as a tourist? Why or why not?

■■■■■■■■■■■■■■■■■■■■■■■■■■■■■ *GO TO* MyEnglishLab *TO GIVE YOUR OPINION ABOUT ANOTHER QUESTION.*

READING TWO   A TRAVEL JOURNAL

READ

1 Look at the boldfaced words and phrases in the reading and think about the questions.

1. Which words or phrases do you know the meaning of?

2. Can you use any of the words or phrases in a sentence?

2 Now read these entries from the journal of a tourist who traveled to Antarctica.

A TRAVEL JOURNAL

Chile, South America
February 16

1   The sunlight was shining so brightly as our plane flew over the snow-covered Andes mountains, which seemed to go on forever.

Cape Horn
February 18

2   We spent the morning at a small church named Star of the Sea. This is a quiet place where visitors are invited to remember the sailors from all over the world who died here. They were all

trying to sail around the southern point of South America, and many of them lost their lives at sea.

3   We were welcomed today by the captain and crew. They gave us warm Antarctic jackets and introduced themselves to us. Sea birds followed the ship closely, sailing in the cold wind. As we headed south, we saw a pink ship in the distance. Our captain explained that it was not a ship but an iceberg[1]—the first one of our trip.

Deception Island, Antarctica
February 21

4   We landed on Bailey Head, where thousands and thousands of penguins greeted us. The crew gave us a set of rules to follow to **protect** the **environment**. Mark, one of the scientists on our ship, asked us to bring him any trash that we find. He is studying the amount of trash created by tourists in Antarctica each year.

5   Tonight we'll listen to Christina, another scientist. She will explain the plant and animal life to us. Then she will show us a DVD on Antarctica.

6   The more I see of this remote place, the more I want to learn.

Cuverville Island, Antarctica
February 23

7   We awakened this morning to the noisy sound of penguins. They're loud! We met a team of biologists living in tents. They are studying the effect of tourists on baby penguins. When our captain invited the biologists to come on board for a hot shower, they joined us immediately. Then we cruised through the icebergs, which appeared in unbelievable shapes and sizes, as the sun was sinking in the sky. They seemed to be works of art by an ice sculptor.[2]

Paradise Bay, Antarctica
February 25

8   Today, we reached the mainland of the **continent**. Our guide today was Stephanie, who helped us walk through snow to a point about 500 feet above sea level. When we reached the top, we laughed like children because it was so much fun to be up there. Later, we explored a glacier[3] in motorized rubber boats. The ice was as thick as the

(continued on next page)

[1] **iceberg:** an extremely large piece of ice floating in the sea
[2] **sculptor:** an artist who makes objects from clay, wood, metal, etc.
[3] **glacier:** a large area of ice that moves slowly over an area of land

crushed ice in a soft drink, but we pushed through it.

9   Because we wanted to celebrate crossing the Antarctic Circle, we drank some champagne today. Not many visitors come this far south! Mark explained an interesting characteristic of the ice down here. It is blue because it catches all the colors of the rainbow except for blue. I have always thought of Antarctica as nothing but white. But now I see a clear blue light shining through the mountains of ice all around us, and I have no words to describe the beauty of this landscape.

10   Our ship passed a huge field of **frozen** sea. Mark invited us to come out and play.

We weren't sure at first, but when we felt how solid it was, we jumped and ran. All around us were mountains and glaciers that no one has ever explored. It amazed me to think that no human hand or foot has ever touched them; only a few human eyes have seen them.

11   Even though it will be hard to describe, I will try to explain this amazing experience to my friends at home. We all felt sad today when we realized that our ship was heading north. We really aren't ready to leave Antarctica, a unique world.

COMPREHENSION

Discuss the questions with the class.

1. How did the writer feel about her trip? What adjectives describe her emotions?

2. What opinion does the writer have about tourism in Antarctica? How do you know?

GO TO MyEnglishLab FOR MORE VOCABULARY PRACTICE.

READING SKILL

1 Read paragraph 3 of Reading Two again. What is the meaning of "captain"? What information before or after this word helps you to understand what it means?

UNDERSTANDING VOCABULARY FROM CONTEXT CLUES

Good readers use **context clues** to understand new vocabulary in a text. Context clues are **other words or phrases** that help you understand the meaning of a word you don't know. Sometimes they come before the word and sometimes they come after the word.

Look at the example and read the explanation:

• "We were welcomed today by the **captain** and crew." *(paragraph 3)*

That sentence comes after the subheading "Drake Passage—aboard the tour ship Explorer." This subheading contains a word that you might already know: **ship**. If you know that *a ship is a boat*, you could guess that *a captain is someone who controls a ship*.

Using context clues helps you understand a passage more quickly and easily.

2 Work with a partner to answer questions about Reading Two. Try to guess the meanings of the words by using context clues.

1. Read **paragraph 7**. What is the meaning of *cruised*?

   a. moved along slowly   **b.** moved along quickly

2. Read **paragraph 8**. What is the meaning of *crushed*?

   a. something is very cold   **b.** something is broken into pieces

3. Read **paragraph 10**. What is the meaning of *solid*?

   a. soft with holes   **b.** hard with no holes

GO TO MyEnglishLab FOR MORE SKILL PRACTICE

STEP 1: Organize

Reading One (**R1**) and Reading Two (**R2**) contain opinions about tourists in Antarctica. This chart compares the views of the scientist with the views of the tourist. Look at the list of opinions below. Place them in the appropriate category by writing the letter of each opinion in the chart.

OPINIONS OF THE SCIENTIST (R1)	OPINIONS OF THE TOURIST (R2)
1. The Antarctic environment must be preserved for research.	1. _____
2. We cannot control the behavior of tourists.	2. _____
3. _____	3. Tourists can actually help scientists with their experiments.
4. Tourists don't care about Antarctica.	4. _____

a. Tourists are interested in learning about Antarctica.

b. Tourists can follow rules made by scientists.

c. Tourists take scientists away from their research, can damage scientific projects, and hurt the environment.

d. As tourists learn about Antarctica and return home to tell their friends and families about its importance, they may want to help preserve the environment of Antarctica.

STEP 2: Synthesize

Imagine that the tourist in Reading Two meets the scientist in Reading One. Work with a partner to complete their dialogue. Use information from the chart in Step 1, but do not copy—try to use your own words. Act out your dialogue.

TOURIST: I understand that you've done some research in Antarctica. I love that place!

SCIENTIST: [*worried*] Have you been there? As a tourist?

TOURIST: Yes. It was the trip of a lifetime.

SCIENTIST: Well, to be honest with you, _____

TOURIST: I understand your concern, but _____

SCIENTIST: _____

TOURIST: _____

GO TO MyEnglishLab TO CHECK WHAT YOU LEARNED.

3 FOCUS ON WRITING

VOCABULARY

REVIEW

Work in a small group. Match the adjectives in the box with the nouns from Reading One and Reading Two surrounding them. List as many possible combinations as you can think of on the lines below.

icebergs   environment

effect   **Adjectives**   beauty

         coastal
         fragile   landscape
sunlight   frozen
         harsh
         natural   consequences
         remote
temperature scientific   continent
         vast

research   glaciers

coastal environment, coastal landscape, _____

_____

_____

_____

_____

_____

_____

_____

EXPAND

Work in pairs. Read the chart. Then analyze the relationships between the vocabulary words given below. First, circle the word that best completes each comparison. Be sure that the second pair of words has a similar relationship to the first pair. Second, label each comparison with the letter of the correct category.

CATEGORY	DEFINITION	EXAMPLE
SYNONYM (S)	The words have a similar meaning.	*work : job*
ANTONYM (A)	The words have opposite meanings.	*harsh : gentle*
CAUSE / EFFECT (C / E)	One word or phrase is the result of another word or phrase.	*oil spill : death of penguins*
DEGREE (D)	One word has a stronger meaning than the other.	*damaged : destroyed*

__S__ 1. *unique : rare* = huge : _____
   a. fragile   b. remote   c.) vast

_____ 2. *heavy rain : flood* = vast ice fields : _____
   a. cooler temperature   b. ozone layer   c. global warming

_____ 3. *protected : preserved* = surprising : _____
   a. temporary   b. amazing   c. fragile

_____ 4. *harsh : comfortable* = inland : _____
   a. coastal   b. global   c. ocean

_____ 5. *ice fields : natural air conditioning* = government : _____
   a. global warming   b. protection   c. environment

_____ 6. *consequence : effect* = traveler : _____
   a. climate   b. tourist   c. researcher

_____ 7. *project : work* = far : _____
   a. harsh   b. remote   c. coastal

_____ 8. *pretty : beautiful* = read : _____
   a. scan   b. predict   c. research

_____ **9.** *careful : controlled* : = delicate : _____

    a. quiet   **b.** fragile   **c.** unbelievable

_____ **10.** *tourists : trash* = scientists : _____

    a. research   **b.** environment   **c.** continents

_____ **11.** *inhabit : live* = beautiful : _____

    a. scenic   **b.** uncrowded   **c.** pleasant

_____ **12.** *uncomfortable : harsh* = cold : _____

    a. hot   **b.** frozen   **c.** ice

CREATE

Think of a place of natural beauty that you have visited. Write sentences using the words in parentheses to describe this place.

1. (harsh) _____

_____

2. (landscape) _____

_____

3. (environment)_____

_____

4. (inhabit) _____

_____

5. (tourists) _____

_____

GO TO MyEnglishLab FOR MORE VOCABULARY PRACTICE.

GRAMMAR

1 Look at the sentences. What do they mean?

- Because Antarctica is the center of important scientific research, it must be preserved.

- Even though I can appreciate tourists' desire to experience this beautiful landscape, I feel Antarctica should be closed to them.

BECAUSE AND EVEN THOUGH	
1. *Because* gives a **reason**.	Main Clause Dependent Clause Antarctica must be preserved *because* it is the center of important scientific research. Dependent Clause Main Clause *Because* Antarctica is beautiful, tourists enjoy it.

2. *Even though* explains an **unexpected result**.
It can also express a **contrast**, or difference. (*Although* can be used in a similar way.)
	Main Clause
	Some scientists in Antarctica do not find
	         Dependent Clause
	answers to their questions *even though* they work very hard. (*unexpected result*)
	Dependent Clause
	Even though some people want to visit
	         Main Clause
	Antarctica, others do not. (*contrast*)

3. Notice that each sentence above has a **main clause** and a **dependent clause**. (A main clause can stand alone. A dependent clause cannot.)

The **dependent clauses** begin with *because* or *even though*. Always use a **comma** after the dependent clause when it begins the sentence.

2 Join each pair of sentences using **because** or **even though**. Add a comma when the dependent clause comes before the main clause.

1. I had to interrupt my research and greet tourists. I was very busy.

   I had to interrupt my research and greet tourists even though I was very busy.

2. I understand why tourists want to see Antarctica. They shouldn't be allowed to visit.

   _____

3. The Earth's temperature is rising. Meteorologists are worried.

   _____

4. Antarctica's unique environment is in danger. There is no government in Antarctica to help preserve it.

_____

5. Tourists enjoy the beauty of Antarctica. They sometimes damage the environment.

_____

6. Scientists are interested in protecting Antarctica's natural environment. Tour companies are not.

_____

7. We had an amazing time on this remote continent. It was difficult to travel in such a harsh environment.

_____

8. Antarctica is unbelievably scenic. Tourists recommend it to their friends.

_____

3 Use your own ideas to complete the sentences using **because** or **even though**. Circle the appropriate verb form.

1. I would / wouldn't like to visit Antarctica _____

_____.

2. _____, tourism should / shouldn't be allowed in Antarctica.

3. Antarctica should / shouldn't be closed to tourists _____

_____.

4. I would / wouldn't like to be a scientific researcher in Antarctica _____

_____.

■■■ GO TO MyEnglishLab TO CHECK WHAT YOU LEARNED.

FINAL WRITING TASK

In this unit, you read an opinion essay written by a scientist and a travel journal written by a tourist. Now imagine that you are a tourist in Antarctica. What is your opinion about tourism there?

You are going to **write an opinion essay from a tourist's point of view**. You will give reasons why Antarctica should be open to tourism. Use the vocabulary and grammar from the unit.*

PREPARE TO WRITE: Listing

1 Look back at "Opinions of the Tourist" in Step I, page 140. Copy these opinions here. Add two more of your own opinions to the list.

1. _____

2. _____

3. _____

4. _____

5. _____

6. _____

2 Share your list with a partner. Do you have different opinions? Discuss them.

---

* For Alternative Writing Topics, see page 151. These topics can be used in place of the writing topic for this unit or as homework. The alternative topics relate to the theme of the unit but may not target the same grammar or rhetorical structures taught in the unit.

WRITE: An Opinion Essay

STRUCTURING AN OPINION ESSAY

An **essay** is a piece of nonfiction writing that has more than one or two paragraphs and is organized around a central idea. An **opinion essay** expresses an opinion about something. There are three important parts of a good opinion essay:

Introductory Paragraph

- It introduces your topic.
- It includes a thesis statement that states the main idea of the essay (your opinion). It is usually the last sentence in the paragraph.

Body (at least one paragraph)

- Each paragraph of the body starts with a topic sentence that states a reason for your opinion.
- It is followed by details that support the reason for your opinion. These supporting details can be facts, examples, or explanations.
  - It can take 100 years for a plant to grow back in Antarctica. *(fact)*
  - Astronomers and biologists are two kinds of scientists who work in Antarctica. *(example)*
  - Antarctica has no government, which means that no one is making sure that penguins, plants, and sea are safe. *(explanation)*

Concluding Paragraph

- It restates the main idea expressed in your thesis statement.

1 Refer to Reading One to complete the tasks.

1. Look at the introductory paragraph. Find the thesis statement. Copy it here.

   _____

2. Underline the topic sentence of each of the body paragraphs.

3. In paragraphs 2, 3, and 4, what types of supporting details are used (facts, examples, or explanations)?

   PARAGRAPH 2: _____

   PARAGRAPH 3: _____

   PARAGRAPH 4: _____

4. Find the concluding sentence that restates the main idea. Write it here.

   _____

2 You are going to write an opinion essay from a tourist's point of view. Your essay will have four paragraphs: an introductory paragraph, two body paragraphs, and a concluding paragraph. In the body, you will give reasons to support your opinion and details to support your reasons. Plan your first draft by completing the outline.

I. **Introductory Paragraph:**

    Thesis Statement (your opinion about tourism):

    _____

    _____

II. **Body Paragraph:**

    Topic Sentence (one reason for your opinion):

    _____

    Supporting Details (facts, examples, or explanations):

    _____

    _____

    _____

III. **Body Paragraph:**

    Topic Sentence (another reason for your opinion):

    _____

    Supporting Details (facts, examples, or explanations):

    _____

    _____

    _____

IV. **Concluding Paragraph:**

    Restatement of thesis (restate your opinion about tourism):

    _____

    _____

    _____

3 Use your outline and your notes to write the first draft of your essay.

REVISE: Choosing Effective Supporting Details

The **supporting details** in your body paragraph should help the reader understand the reasons for your opinion. Effective supporting details may include **facts, examples,** or **explanations**.

1 Read an essay about tourism on Cape Cod. The underlined supporting details in the body paragraph are weak because they do not provide facts, examples, or explanations to support the reasons for the writer's opinion.

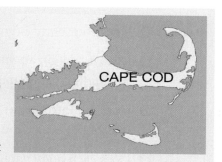

My family lives on Cape Cod in Massachusetts. Cape Cod is a long piece of land that goes out into the Atlantic Ocean. There are beaches on two sides. It is a beautiful place, but there is too much tourism. I think Cape Cod should be closed to tourists.

Tourism is hurting Cape Cod in several ways. First, there are not many good jobs for people on Cape Cod. (**a**) The jobs don't pay well. In addition, living on Cape Cod during the summer is very expensive. (**b**) Everything is expensive. Finally, tourists hurt the environment. (**c**) There are too many people.

I would like to live on Cape Cod for the rest of my life. However, I will have to leave if so many tourists visit each summer. That's why I believe that tourism is not good for Cape Cod.

2 The supporting details below are stronger because they include more specific information. Work with a partner. Read the details. Decide which details should replace the underlined weak details in the essay in Exercise 1. Write the appropriate letter next to each detail.

_____ **1.** About 6 million people visit Cape Cod each year. These people bring their cars, so there is a lot of traffic. They crowd the beaches and pollute the ocean.

_____ **2.** Most jobs are in hotels, restaurants, or souvenir shops. These jobs have low pay and require very hard work.

_____ **3.** The cost of living is higher for both tourists and people who live in the Cape year-round. The prices of gas, groceries, and entertainment all increase.

3 What kinds of supporting details do the new sections contain: facts, examples, or explanations? Do you think the details are effective? Why or why not?

4 Go back to the first draft of your essay. Are the supporting details effective? Do they include facts, examples, and explanations that make the ideas clear? If not, make the appropriate revisions.

Go to MyEnglishLab and write the final draft of your essay. Carefully edit it for grammatical and mechanical errors, such as spelling, capitalization, and punctuation. Make sure you use some of the vocabulary and grammar from the unit. Use the checklist to help you write your final draft. Then submit your essay to your teacher.

FINAL DRAFT CHECKLIST

❏ Does your essay express your opinion about how tourism can help Antarctica?

❏ Does it contain an introductory paragraph, two body paragraphs, and a concluding paragraph?

❏ Does the introductory paragraph contain a thesis statement stating the main idea of the essay (your opinion)?

❏ Does each body paragraph contain a topic sentence stating the main idea of the paragraph (a reason for your opinion)?

❏ Does each body paragraph contain at least two details supporting the reason for your opinion?

❏ Are the details facts, examples, or explanations?

❏ Does the concluding paragraph restate the main idea expressed in the thesis statement?

❏ Are the *because* and *even though* clauses used correctly?

❏ Do these clauses have the correct punctuation?

❏ Do you use new vocabulary from the unit?

UNIT PROJECT

Investigate tourism in the Arctic. Write a letter to an organization protecting the Arctic environment. Share what you learn with your classmates. Follow these steps:

STEP 1: Go to a travel agency or use the Internet to get information about visiting the Arctic.

STEP 2: Use the Internet or go to the library to find the name of a local, national, or international organization that is working to protect the Arctic environment. Write to the organization and ask these questions:

- Have any accidents occurred because of tourists?

- How have local people responded to tourists? Are they happy to have visitors?

- Is the Arctic ecosystem* endangered in any way because of the presence of tourists?

STEP 3: Share the letter you receive with the class.

ALTERNATIVE WRITING TOPICS

Write about one of the topics. Use the vocabulary and grammar from the unit.

1. What are the advantages and disadvantages of living in a remote area? Would you like to live in a remote area? Why or why not? Write an essay explaining your opinion.

2. With all the human suffering in the world, is it still important to protect plants and animals? Why? Write an essay giving your opinion about this topic.

■■■■■■■■■■■■■■■■■■■■■■■■■■ *GO TO* MyEnglishLab *TO WRITE ABOUT ONE OF THE ALTERNATIVE TOPICS, WATCH A VIDEO ABOUT ECOTOURISM, AND TAKE THE UNIT 6 ACHIEVEMENT TEST.* ■■■■■■■■■■■■■■■■■■■■

---

* **ecosystem:** all the animals and plants in a particular area and the way in which they are related to each other and to the environment

FINDING A
Spouse

1. Do you know which culture is represented in the photograph? Is this ceremony similar to or different from marriage ceremonies in your home culture?

2. Some people marry for love. Others marry for money. What are other reasons people marry?

3. What are some characteristics of a happy marriage?

GO TO MyEnglishLab TO CHECK WHAT YOU KNOW.

2 FOCUS ON READING

VOCABULARY

1 Work in a small group. Take this quiz—just for fun! Test your knowledge of past and present marriage customs around the world. Look at the list of cultures in the box. Choose one or more cultures that you think have practiced the custom described in each sentence. Write the letters on the line. Pay attention to the boldfaced words.

a. Arab	**d.** traditional Vietnamese	**g.** modern European
b. old Bavarian	**e.** traditional Chinese	**h.** early Mormon
c. traditional Hopi	**f.** Oneida Community (American, 1800s)	

_a, d, e_ **1.** Parents try to find someone who has the right **background**, someone who has gone to school and who has an honorable mother and father.

_____ **2.** Girls are allowed to choose a marriage partner. Their favorite boyfriend can become their spouse.

_____ **3.** Parents use a matchmaker to find a spouse with the right characteristics, for example, someone who is honest, intelligent, and hard-working.

_____ **4.** Men and women can usually follow their romantic feelings and get married for love rather than just the advice from their parents.

_____ **5.** The goal of marriage is to produce sons, and these sons will take on a leadership position by making the important decisions for the family.

_____ **6.** If a woman can become pregnant, the man will ask her to marry him. Having children is very important.

_____ **7.** Getting pregnant before marriage is acceptable because it allows a woman to show the community her fertility.

_____ **8.** All the people in the community raise the children, not just the mother and father.

_____ **9.** This group practices polygamy, following the example of their leader, Joseph Smith.

2 Match the words on the left with the definitions on the right.

_b_   **1. background**

_____   **2. spouse**

_____   **3. characteristics**

_____   **4. romantic**

_____   **5. produce**

_____   **6. leadership**

_____   **7. pregnant**

_____   **8. fertility**

_____   **9. raise**

_____   **10. polygamy**

a. having a baby that has not been born yet growing in your body

~~**b.** past experience, including family life and education~~

c. to take care of and educate

d. the custom of having more than one wife at a time

e. the ability to have children

f. the ability to direct other people

g. related to strong feelings of love between two people

h. special features or qualities that make each person or thing different from others

i. a husband or wife

j. to make or create

▪▪▪▪▪▪▪▪▪▪▪▪▪▪▪▪▪▪▪▪▪▪▪▪▪▪▪▪▪▪▪▪▪▪▪▪ GO TO MyEnglishLab FOR MORE VOCABULARY PRACTICE.

PREVIEW

The following article comes from a journal for students of anthropology (the study of how human beings live together in communities). Read the title and first paragraph. What do you think the article will focus on? Check (✓) your answer.

_____ **a.** problems that occur after marriage

_____ **b.** things people do before marriage

_____ **c.** different cultural backgrounds

Now read the rest of the article.

Finding a Spouse

1   Human beings are born into families, and most families begin with the joining together of a man and a woman in marriage. All societies have their own form of marriage. The ideas that we have about marriage are part of our cultural **background**; they are part of our basic beliefs about right and wrong. As we study marriage, we find that different cultures have solved the problem of finding a **spouse** in different ways. Finding a marriage partner has never been easy for people, no matter when or where they have lived.

2   In traditional Chinese culture, marriage decisions were made by parents for their children. Parents who wanted to find a spouse for their son or daughter asked a matchmaker to find someone with the right **characteristics**, including age and educational background. According to the Chinese way of thinking, it would be a serious mistake to allow two young people to follow their **romantic** feelings and choose their own partners. The all-important decision of marriage was made by older family members who understood that the goal of marriage was to **produce** healthy sons. In traditional Chinese society, sons were important because they would take positions of **leadership** in the family and keep the family name alive.

3   As part of our cultural background, beliefs about marriage can be as different as the cultures of the world. While the traditional Chinese did not believe that young people should be free to choose their own marriage partners, the Hopi, a native people of North America, had a very different idea about freedom. The Hopi allowed boys to leave their parents' home at age thirteen to live in a kiva, a special home for young males. There they enjoyed the freedom to go out alone at night and secretly visit young girls. Most boys tried to leave the girl's home before daylight, but a girl's parents usually did not get angry about the night visits. They allowed the visits to continue if they were impressed that the boy was someone who would make a good marriage partner. After a few months of receiving visits, most girls became **pregnant**. As a consequence, they could choose their favorite boy for a husband.

4   The Hopi culture is not the only one that allowed young people to visit each other at night. Some Bavarian people of southern Germany once had a "windowing" custom that took place when young women left their windows open at night so that young men could enter their bedrooms. When a woman became pregnant, the man usually asked her to marry him. But women who did not manage to get pregnant after windowing were often unable to find a husband. This was because **fertility** was a very

important requirement for women in this culture, and the windowing custom allowed them to prove their fertility to others in the community. Some people are surprised when they learn of this unique custom because they expect the people of southern Germany to follow the rules of the Catholic religion, which teach that it is wrong for unmarried women to become pregnant. But the windowing custom is only one example of the surprising views of marriage that are found around the world, even among people whose religious beliefs require more common marriage practices.

5   One view of marriage that surprises most of us today was held by John Noyes, a religious man who started the Oneida Community in the state of New York in 1831. He began it as an experiment of a different way of living. Noyes decided that group marriage was the best way for men and women to live together. In this form of marriage, men and women changed partners frequently. They were expected to love all members of the community equally. Children belonged to all members of the community, and all the adults worked hard to support themselves and shared everything they had. Members of the Oneida Community succeeded in this lifestyle for a while without any serious problems; however, this way of life ended when John Noyes left the community in 1876. Without his leadership and unique way of thinking, members of the community quickly returned to the traditional marriage of one woman and one man.

6   A more famous example of a different style of marriage is found among the early Mormons—a Christian sect that was founded in New York State in 1830 and migrated to Utah in 1847. The group's first leader, Joseph Smith, believed in **polygamy**. As the Mormon church grew, many of the men followed Smith's teaching and married a number of wives. The Mormons believed that it was a woman's duty to marry at a young age and **raise** as many children as possible. For example, in 1854, one Mormon leader became a father nine times in one week when nine of his wives all had babies. In 1890, however, polygamy was officially banned by the church. Today, while the Mormon church teaches that marriage should be a partnership of one man and one woman, there are some smaller groups which have left the main group and still practice polygamy.

7   In these modern times, there are some men who might agree with the custom of allowing a man to have as many wives as he chooses. Many young lovers today dream of the freedom of the Hopi, and some of us wish that a matchmaker would help us find the perfect mate. Finding a spouse with whom we can commit to spending a lifetime has always been an important concern. Despite all the different ways of finding a marriage partner, one idea is the same throughout the world: Marriage is a basic and important part of human life.

MAIN IDEAS

1 Look again at the Preview on page 155. Was your prediction correct?

2 Work in a small group. These sentences state cultural beliefs. Match each belief with the correct culture.

a. traditional Hopi	**c.** Oneida Community	**e.** early Mormon
b. old Bavarian	**d.** traditional Chinese	

_____ **1.** Young people are not capable of making the right marriage choices for themselves.

_____ **2.** Getting pregnant shows that you will be a good wife.

_____ **3.** Women should have as many children as possible.

_____ **4.** A girl should be free to choose her own husband.

_____ **5.** It is better for society if people are not limited to one marriage partner.

DETAILS

Write short answers to the questions. Share your answers with a classmate.

1. Who helped Chinese parents choose a spouse for their sons or daughters? How did this person help?

_____

2. What was the Chinese idea of a successful marriage?

_____

3. At what age did young Hopi boys leave their homes?

_____

4. Why did Hopi parents sometimes stop night visits?

_____

5. How did Bavarian women find a husband?

_____

6. What happened to a woman in Bavaria if she did not become pregnant?

_____

7. What do people in some Catholic countries believe about unmarried women?

_____

8. Why didn't the Oneida Community continue to exist?

_____

9. What happened to the Mormon church in 1890?

_____

MAKE INFERENCES

INFERRING DEGREE

An **inference** is an **educated guess** about something that is **not directly stated** in a text.

Writers sometimes **suggest the degree** of something (that is, if something is **more or less than** something else) without directly stating it. A strong reader can **infer** that **degree** by reading the text closely.

Look at the example and read the explanation.

- In some cultures, the marriage decision was made freely by young people. In other cultures, the marriage decision was not made as freely.

Rate the degree of freedom young people had in choosing a spouse. Circle a number from 1 to 5. (1 = least freedom and 5 = most freedom)

a. How much freedom did young people in the Bavarian culture have?   1 2 3 4 5
b. How much freedom did young people in the Hopi culture have?   1 2 3 4 5

a: The best answer is 3, which indicates a somewhat limited degree of freedom.
In **paragraph 4**, we learn that Bavarian women who did not prove their fertility by getting pregnant were unable to find a spouse. Their freedom was limited by their fertility.

b: The best answer is 4, which indicates an almost unlimited degree of freedom.
In **paragraph 3**, we learn that Hopi girls could choose their favorite visitor as a husband. They did not have to prove their fertility to the community. Girls were allowed to receive visits as long as their parents believed that the visiting boys would be good husbands.

After reading the text closely, we can **infer** that young Bavarians had **less** freedom to choose a spouse than young Hopis.

Rate the degree of freedom that young people had in choosing a spouse in the cultures mentioned in Reading One. Circle a number from 1–5 (1 = least freedom and 5 = most freedom). Refer to the paragraphs in parentheses.

a. old Bavarian *(paragraph 4)*   1 2 ③ 4 5

b. traditional Hopi *(paragraph 3)*   1 2 3 ④ 5

c. traditional Chinese *(paragraph 2)*   1 2 3 4 5

d. early Mormon *(paragraph 6)*   1 2 3 4 5

e. Oneida Community *(paragraph 5)*   1 2 3 4 5

Now discuss your answers with a partner. Point out the sentences, words, or phrases in the paragraphs that helped you find the answers.

EXPRESS OPINIONS

Work in groups of three. Discuss the pros and cons of each marriage custom. Then choose one person in your group to report the ideas to the class.

Marriage Customs:

- arranged by parents
- girls choosing their favorite boy after becoming pregnant
- the "windowing" custom
- group marriage
- one man having multiple wives
- choosing your own spouse because you are in love with him or her

■■■■■■■■■■■■■■■■■■■■■■■■■■■■■■■■■ GO TO MyEnglishLab TO GIVE YOUR OPINION ABOUT ANOTHER SUBJECT.

READING TWO   WHAT'S WRONG WITH TRADITION?

READ

1 Look at the boldfaced words and phrases in the reading and think about the questions.

1. Which words or phrases do you know the meanings of?

2. Can you use any of the words or phrases in a sentence?

2 Now read the letter to the editor from the student newspaper of an American university. It was written by an international student who believes strongly in his culture's traditional way of choosing a spouse.

"What's Wrong with Tradition?"

Dear Editor:

1   I am a 27-year-old student from Vietnam. My purpose in coming here is to get a business degree. I am extremely grateful to have the chance to get an education in a country of such great business leadership. However, I am tired of the questions that people ask me about my personal life. American students seem to think that their way of dating romantically before marriage is the only way, but I disagree. Let me give you an example from my own life.

2   My parents have been married for 35 years. Their marriage has all the characteristics of a happy one: deep friendship, love, and trust. They have six children, and I am the second son. Because of their help, I am able to study in the United States. They have always worked hard to raise their children in the right way and help them become good people. When I finish my degree, I will go back to my country and help my parents, just like they have helped me. This makes me think of our family life as a golden ring, something I am proud of. Because of my parents' example, I believe in **monogamy** for life.

3   American people are always **shocked** when I tell them that my parents met for the first time on their wedding day. Americans can't believe that an **arranged marriage** could be happy, but I have seen my parents with my own eyes. They love each other faithfully, and they are proud of the children that their marriage has produced. They learned to love each other slowly, as time passed. I believe they share a true and **everlasting** love.

4   When people ask, "Are you looking for a girlfriend?" I tell them no. For me, studying comes first. When I go back to my country and start working, my parents will help me find a good wife. She will be someone with a good family background, someone I can trust. She will be my one and only wife. Good apples come from good trees. If I marry a good apple, we can make a beautiful, growing tree together: no divorce, no AIDS, no broken heart.

5   I want a peaceful, happy life just like my parents have. Why can't Americans understand this?

Paul Nguyen

COMPREHENSION

Read the statements and mark them **T** (true) or **F** (false). Rewrite the false statements to make them true.

_____ **1.** Paul Nguyen thinks dating romantically is the best way to find a marriage partner.

_____ **2.** Paul thinks a happy marriage includes deep friendship, love, and trust.

_____ **3.** His parents were in love with each other before the marriage.

_____ **4.** Paul wants a different life from that of his parents.

_____ **5.** Paul thinks his parents can help find him a good wife.

GO TO MyEnglishLab FOR MORE VOCABULARY PRACTICE.

READING SKILL

1 Read Paragraph 4 of Reading Two again. What is the meaning of the statement "Good apples come from good trees"? What information in the paragraph is this related to? Underline the sentences that give information about the meaning of the "good apples" statement.

UNDERSTANDING METAPHORS

Writers use metaphors to make their ideas more interesting. A **metaphor** is a **word picture** that **relates an idea to something in the real world**. Metaphors can either be followed or preceded by details that make their meaning clear.

Look at the example and read the explanation:

- "Good apples come from good trees."

The statement "Good apples come from good trees" follows the description of "someone with a good family background, someone I can trust." A person's family background can be compared to a tree. If a tree is healthy and well cared for, it will produce good fruit.
The writer adds details to show the "good fruit" that comes from having a good family background: "no divorce, no AIDS, no broken heart."

2 Look at the "golden ring" metaphor in paragraph 2. What details precede this metaphor?

3 Which characteristics of a "golden ring" are closely related to these details? Check (√) two.

_____ **a.** A golden ring is small.

_____ **b.** A golden ring is valuable.

_____ **c.** A golden ring can be lost.

_____ **d.** A golden ring is a circle that goes on and on.

▪▪ *GO TO* MyEnglishLab *FOR MORE SKILL PRACTICE.*

CONNECT THE READINGS

STEP 1: Organize

Reading One (**R1**) and Reading Two (**R2**) contain information about the different ways of finding a spouse. Choose the letter of the best ending on the right to complete each sentence on the left.

1. Traditional Chinese believed that parents __C__.

a. practiced polygamy

2. According to the Hopi, young people _____.

b. help people share spouses as a community

3. In old Bavarian culture, pregnancy before marriage _____.

~~**c.** could make better marriage choices than young people~~

4. The Oneida Community goal was to _____.

d. are able to find partners for themselves

5. Early Mormon couples sometimes _____.

e. is not the best way to find a partner

6. For some Vietnamese, dating _____.

f. was accepted

Imagine that you are taking a sociology class. Your professor has asked you to summarize the different ways of finding a spouse in the cultures mentioned in Reading One and Reading Two. Use information from Step 1 to complete the summary.

ARRANGED MARRIAGE

Culture 1: Traditional Chinese
Culture 2: _____

In an arranged marriage culture, _____ are responsible for choosing a spouse for their children. In some cases, a matchmaker is used. _____ is not considered a good way to find a spouse in an arranged marriage culture.

FERTILITY-BASED MARRIAGE

Culture 1: Traditional Hopi
Culture 2: _____

In a fertility-based marriage culture, people may decide to get married when the female becomes pregnant. _____ are allowed to follow romantic feelings and find their own partners. The ability to _____ is highly valued as proof of fertility.

PLURAL MARRIAGE

Culture 1: Oneida Community
Culture 2: _____

In a plural marriage culture, a person is married to more than one spouse. A common form is _____, which occurs when a man has more than one wife. A less common form is group marriage, which occurs when all members of a group share partners as a _____.

GO TO MyEnglishLab TO CHECK WHAT YOU LEARNED.

VOCABULARY

Read the paragraph about traditional courtship. Then, decide if the sentences are related to courtship (**C**), the wedding ceremony (**W**), or married life (**M**), and mark them appropriately. Share your choices with the class.

> **Courtship** refers to the period of time when a man and a woman get to know each other before
>
> marriage. In some cultures, they spend time together alone. In other cultures, they spend time
>
> together with friends and relatives. During this time, a couple may decide whether or not to marry,
>
> or the decision is made for them by parents.

___W___ **1.** Members of the community are invited to watch the couple promise to love each other faithfully with an **everlasting** love.

_____ **2.** The man surprises the woman with flowers to show his **romantic** feelings for the first time.

_____ **3.** The wife and mother-in-law disagree about the best way to **raise** the two sons.

_____ **4.** Friends and relatives throw rice at the couple to make a wish for their **fertility**.

_____ **5.** No one is **shocked** when a husband and wife meet for the first time on their wedding day.

_____ **6.** The husband and wife hope that their marriage will **produce** healthy children.

_____ **7.** A man and a woman are attracted to each other and choose to spend time together because of such **characteristics** as good looks, intelligence, and kindness. Little by little, each person discovers more about the other's **background**.

_____ **8.** Important words are spoken by a person in a position of **leadership**.

_____ **9.** The woman happily tells her mother that she is **pregnant**.

_____ **10.** The man realizes that the woman will be an excellent **spouse**.

_____ **11.** The parents look at the age and educational background of a possible husband for their daughter in an **arranged marriage**.

(continued on next page)

_____ **12.** The man and woman enter a life of **monogamy** as they become "man and wife" in front of others.

_____ **13.** In previous times, Mormons practiced **polygamy** so that they could have as many children as possible.

EXPAND

Work in pairs. Read the chart. Then analyze the relationships between the vocabulary words given below. First, circle the word that best completes each comparison. Be sure that the second pair of words has a similar relationship to the first pair. Second, label each comparison with the letter of the correct category.

CATEGORY	DEFINITION	EXAMPLE
SYNONYM (S)	The words have a very similar meaning.	*mistake : error*
ANTONYM (A)	The words have opposite meanings.	*modern : traditional*
CAUSE / EFFECT (C / E)	One word is the result of another word.	*mistakes : experience*
DEGREE (D)	One word has a stronger meaning than the other.	*different : unique*

__S__ **1.** *characteristics : features* = make : _____
    a. raise   **(b.)** produce   **c.** grow

_____ **2.** *marriage : divorce* = pregnancy : _____
    a. infertility   **b.** commitment   **c.** traditional

_____ **3.** *pregnancy : baby* = romance : _____
    a. love marriage   **b.** arranged marriage   **c.** group marriage

_____ **4.** *surprised : shocked* = enduring : _____
    a. lasting   **b.** continuing   **c.** everlasting

_____ **5.** *usually : always* = romantic : _____
    a. loving   **b.** temporary   **c.** valuable

_____ **6.** *engagement : marriage* = fertility : _____
    a. miracle   **b.** proof   **c.** pregnancy

_____ **7.** *custom : tradition* = society : _____
    a. background   **b.** culture   **c.** organization

_____ **8.** *honesty : dishonesty* = monogamy : _____

        a. monopoly   **b.** faithfulness   **c.** polygamy

_____ **9.** *faith : religion* = support : _____

        a. produce   **b.** take care of   **c.** help

_____ **10.** *wife : husband* = bride : _____

        a. partner   **b.** spouse   **c.** groom

CREATE

Describe five different marriage traditions in your culture. Write one or two paragraphs using at least five of these words.

arranged marriage	custom	fertility	romantic
attracted to	engagement	leadership	shocked
background	everlasting	modern	spouse
characteristics	faithfully	monogamy	traditional

GO TO MyEnglishLab *FOR MORE VOCABULARY PRACTICE.*

GRAMMAR

1 Look at this passage from "Finding a Spouse." Underline the definite articles (*the*). Circle the indefinite articles (*a/an*).

A more famous example of a different style of marriage is found among the early Mormons—a Christian sect that was founded in New York State in 1830 and migrated to Utah in 1847. The group's first leader, Joseph Smith, believed in polygamy. As the Mormon church grew, many of the men followed Smith's teaching and married a number of wives. The Mormons believed that it was a woman's duty to marry at a young age and raise as many children as possible. For example, in 1854, one Mormon leader became a father nine times in one week when nine of his wives all had babies. In 1890, however, polygamy was officially banned by the church. Today, while the Mormon church teaches that marriage should be a partnership of one man and one woman, there are some smaller groups which have left the main group and still practice polygamy.

DEFINITE AND INDEFINITE ARTICLES

1. Use the **definite article** *the* when you have a specific person, place, or thing in mind. You can use *the* before singular count nouns, plural count nouns, and non-count nouns.	**The** group's first leader, Joseph Smith, believed in polygamy. As **the** Mormon church grew, many of **the** men followed Smith's teaching and married a number of wives.
2. Use the **indefinite article** *a* when you do not have a specific person, place, or thing in mind. Use the **indefinite article** *an* before words that begin with vowel sounds.	He began it as **an** experiment of **a** different way of living.
3. Use the indefinite article *a* the first time you mention a person, place, or thing. Then use the definite article *the* when you refer to that same thing again.	Some Bavarian people of southern Germany once had **a** "windowing" custom that . . . . . . and **the** windowing custom allowed them to prove their fertility to others in the community.
4. Use the definite article *the* in forming the **superlative** of an adjective.	Noyes decided that group marriage was **the** **best** way for men and women to live together.

2 Complete the paragraph with the definite article **the** or the indefinite article **a(n)**.

Planning a Wedding

An American bride often looks in _____ bridal magazine for advice about
                                          1.

planning her wedding. Every bride has her own idea of _____ most perfect
                                                              2.

wedding. For most brides, this includes flowers, music, and _____ delicious
                                                                    3.

wedding cake. Most magazines also provide information about planning _____
                                                                            4.

romantic trip. Some brides dream of going to _____ warm beach, while others
                                                      5.

wish to travel to _____ distant country. Bridal magazines also give advice about
                          6.

following traditional American wedding customs. For example, _____ bride
                                                                    7.

will sometimes give _____ piece of wedding cake to her friends. Each friend
                            8.

takes _____ piece of cake home and places it in a bag underneath her pillow.
              9.

According to tradition, if a woman does this, she will dream of her future husband that night.

_____ woman will see his face in her dreams.
        10.

3 Read each statement, paying special attention to the boldfaced phrase. Then circle the correct explanation of its meaning.

1. I went to **a wedding** last week.

   a. We don't know exactly which wedding.

   b. We know exactly which wedding.

2. **The bride** carried beautiful roses.

   a. This is a specific bride.

   b. This is not a specific bride.

3. The groom wore **a black hat**.

   a. We know exactly which hat.

   b. We don't know exactly which hat.

4. **The hat** reminded me of one I'd seen in movies.

   a. This is the same hat mentioned before.

   b. This is a different hat.

4 Write a paragraph about a wedding that you have attended. Be careful with the use of **the** and **a(n)**. Share your paragraph with a classmate.

GO TO MyEnglishLab *TO CHECK WHAT YOU LEARNED.*

FINAL WRITING TASK

In this unit, you read an article about world customs related to finding a spouse. You also read a letter in support of parents helping their children find a spouse.

Now you are going to **write an essay about the characteristics that you think are important in a spouse or partner**. Use the vocabulary and grammar from the unit.*

---

* For Alternative Writing Topics, see page 175. These topics can be used in place of the writing topic for this unit or as homework. The alternative topics relate to the theme of the unit but may not target the same grammar or rhetorical structures that are taught in the unit.

PREPARE TO WRITE: Categorizing

Categorizing is a way of organizing your ideas by putting them into **logical groups**.

1 In a small group, think of characteristics that are important in a spouse or partner. Have one person in the group write down all the ideas. Think of as many ideas as you can.

Example

athletic	honest	nice smile	wealthy
good-looking	kind	religious	well-educated

2 Choose the characteristics from the list in Exercise 1 that are most important to you. Put these characteristics into categories such as appearance, personality, beliefs, family background, and education / occupation.

Example

Appearance	Personality
nice smile	honest
tall	kind

3 Check (✓) the two categories from Exercise 2 that are most important to you. Check (✓) the three most important characteristics in each category.

WRITE: A Point-by-Point Paragraph

In **point-by-point organization**, the **points (ideas)** in a paragraph are **discussed one by one**. In this essay, each paragraph you write will describe one category, or group, of characteristics that are important in a spouse or partner (personality, background, education, and so on). You will discuss the characteristics in each category one by one.

1 Read the paragraph. Then discuss the questions with a classmate.

My spouse's personality is very important to me. Most importantly, I want to marry someone who is kind. Kindness is important because it affects everyone in the family. It is difficult to live with someone who is mean or critical of others. This is especially important if we have children. It is also important for my spouse to be honest. I want my spouse to tell me the truth. I don't want to be married to someone who hides things from me. Finally, my spouse should have a good sense of humor. I believe that life is easier and more fun with laughter. Even when bad things happen, we should find a way to laugh. For all these reasons, my spouse's personality matters a lot to me.

1. What is the topic sentence? Underline it.

2. What category is discussed in the paragraph?

3. What characteristics are included in that category?

4. What reasons does the writer give for choosing each characteristic?

2 In point-by-point organization, some points may be more important than others. Writers use **transition words** to show the degree of importance. Look at the paragraph in Exercise 1 again. Notice the transition words *most importantly, also,* and *finally* that introduce each characteristic. Which characteristic is most important to the writer?

3 Look back at your list of categories and characteristics in Prepare to Write (see page 170). Number the characteristics in each category by order of importance. Then make notes on your reasons for choosing these characteristics.

4 Use your list from Prepare to Write (page 170) and your notes from this section to write the first draft of your essay. Include the following:

- **an introductory paragraph** including a thesis statement about what is important to you in choosing a spouse or partner

- **two or three body paragraphs**, each one focusing on one category of characteristics (personality, background, beliefs, and so on); plus reasons and examples to describe each characteristic

- **a concluding paragraph** summarizing your main ideas and adding a final comment

REVISE: Using Related Word Forms for Cohesion

In a well-written text, the ideas are cohesive; that is, they fit together clearly. When your **ideas fit together clearly**, you are using **cohesion**.

1 Look at these paragraphs about marriage. Can you identify what makes them cohesive?

1   Some people are surprised when they learn of this unique custom because they expect the

people of southern Germany to follow the rules of the Catholic religion, which teach that it

is wrong for unmarried women to become pregnant. But the windowing custom is only one

example of the surprising views of marriage that are found around the world, even among

people whose religious beliefs require more common marriage practices.

(continued on next page)

2   A more famous example of a different style of marriage is found among the early
Mormons—a Christian sect that was founded in New York State in 1830 and migrated to
Utah in 1847. The group's first leader, Joseph Smith, believed in polygamy. As the Mormon
church grew, many of the men followed Smith's teaching and married a number of wives.
The Mormons believed that it was a woman's duty to marry at a young age and raise as
many children as possible. For example, in 1854, one Mormon leader became a father nine
times in one week when nine of his wives all had babies. In 1890, however, polygamy was
officially banned by the church. Today, while the Mormon church teaches that marriage
should be a partnership of one man and one woman, there are some smaller groups which
have left the main group and still practice polygamy.

Writers use **related word forms** to gain more **cohesion** in their writing.

- In **paragraph 1**, the ideas fit together clearly because the writer uses such related word forms as *religion* and *religious*, *unmarried*, and *marriage*.
- In **paragraph 2**, some related word forms are *marriage, married, marry*. There are also many repetitions of the words *Mormon* and *wives*.

COHESION

The use of **related word forms** helps the writer move smoothly from one idea to the next. The writer is able to keep the reader's focus on the main idea without repeating the same exact words again and again. Look at this example:

- Other pregnant women believe that they are quite **beautiful** during pregnancy. Their **beauty** comes from the joy of becoming a mother. There is a light in their eyes, and their skin shines **beautifully**.

2 Complete the paragraph with the appropriate word forms. Choose words from the box.

court	marriage	romance	~~similar~~	tradition
courtship	married	romantic	similarity	traditional

Many social scientists agree that it is important to marry someone whose background is

_____similar_____, to your own. One example of this idea is expressed when Americans
　　　　1.

talk about marrying "the boy (or girl) next door." When we get _____ to the
　　　　　　　　　　　　　　　　　　　　　　　　　　　　　　　　　　　　　2.

boy or girl next door, we are joining our lives with a partner who shares our lifestyle, income,

and educational level. According to most social scientists, this type of _____
　　3.

is likely to be successful because the spouses will understand each other more easily. One

practical advantage of marrying the boy or girl next door is that it is easy to _____
　　4.

someone who lives near you. During the _____ period, the two partners can
　　　　　　　　　　　　　　　　　　　　5.

get together easily. If they come from _____ families, their parents can watch
　　　　　　　　　　　　　　　　　　　6.

their relationship develop and give them advice. Of course, there is also the possibility that the

_____ will not be accepted by the parents, and the young couple may not be able
　　　　7.

to participate in the _____ of having a wedding ceremony. They may elope, or run
　　　　　　　　　　　8.

away to get married secretly. For some couples, this is a _____ way to begin their
　　　　　　　　　　　　　　　　　　　　　　　　　　　　　9.

lives together. But whether or not they elope, many experts believe that people who marry the boy

or girl next door will be happy. This is because of the _____ of their backgrounds.
　　　　　　　　　　　　　　　　　　　　　　　　　　　10.

3 Go back to the first draft of your essay. Find at least one place in each paragraph where
you can use related word forms to give your writing more cohesion.

GO TO MyEnglishLab FOR MORE SKILL PRACTICE.

EDIT: Writing the Final Draft

Go to MyEnglishLab and write the final draft of your essay. Carefully edit it for grammatical and mechanical errors, such as spelling, capitalization, and punctuation. Make sure you use some of the vocabulary and grammar from the unit. Use the checklist to help you write your final draft. Then submit your essay to your teacher.

FINAL DRAFT CHECKLIST

❏ Does your essay clearly describe the characteristics that you think are important in a spouse or partner?

❏ Does it contain an introductory paragraph, two or three body paragraphs, and a concluding paragraph?

❏ Does the introductory paragraph contain a thesis statement stating the main idea of the essay?

❏ Does each body paragraph focus on one category of characteristics?

❏ Does each body paragraph contain reasons and examples describing the importance of each characteristic?

❏ Does the concluding paragraph restate the main idea expressed in the thesis statement?

❏ Does your essay use related word forms for cohesion?

❏ Do you use definite and indefinite articles correctly?

❏ Do you use new vocabulary from the unit?

UNIT PROJECT

Work with a partner. Research changing marriage statistics around the world. Choose a country to research. Follow these steps:

STEP I: Conduct research on the Internet. Fill in the following information:

Name of country: _____

   1. Percentage of young people who marry now _____

   2. Average age of marriage _____

   3. Percentage of young people who married 10 years ago _____

   4. Percentage of divorces today _____

5. Percentage of couples living together without getting married _____

6. Number of children born to couples who do not marry _____

7. Common ways of finding a spouse:

   - _____

   - _____

   - _____

STEP 2: Present your findings to the class.

STEP 3: Use these questions as a guide to write a summary of the class research.

   - In which countries are the numbers of marriages increasing?
   - In which countries are the numbers of marriages decreasing?
   - Are marriage patterns changing around the world? If so, why?
   - What are the main reasons for people to marry or *not* to marry?
   - What effects are changing marriage customs having on society?

ALTERNATIVE WRITING TOPICS

Write about one of the topics. Use the vocabulary and grammar from the unit.

1. What are the characteristics of a happy marriage? Do these characteristics change as a couple gets older? Write an essay to explain. Describe the happy marriage of a couple that you know. What is special about it?

2. Do you believe that using a matchmaker (including online services) can be a good way to find a spouse or partner? Why or why not? Write an essay to explain. Give reasons to support your opinion.

3. You are taking a quiz in your sociology class. This is one of the questions: Describe a marriage or courtship custom with which you are familiar. How is this custom related to religion and/or traditions? Write an essay to answer the question.

■■■■■■■■■■■■■■■■■■■■■■■■■■■■■■ *GO TO* MyEnglishLab *TO WRITE ABOUT ONE OF THE ALTERNATIVE TOPICS, WATCH A VIDEO ABOUT MARRIAGE, AND TAKE THE UNIT 7 ACHIEVEMENT TEST.* ■■■■■■■■■■■■■■■■■■■■■■■■■

IS OUR CLIMATE Changing?

1 FOCUS ON THE TOPIC

1. What are some ways in which the Earth is changing?

2. How responsible are humans for changes on the planet?

3. Are these changes making the world better or worse?

GO TO MyEnglishLab TO CHECK WHAT YOU KNOW.

VOCABULARY

1 Look at the pictures and read the texts. Pay attention to the boldfaced words.

How Greenhouse Gases Cause Climate Change

Most of the sun's heat hits the Earth and **escapes** back into space. Some is trapped by the **atmosphere** and warms the Earth.

Fossil fuels (coal, gasoline) are burned and **carbon dioxide** (CO_2) is released. Released CO_2 and other **gases** are called greenhouse gas **emissions**.

Greenhouse gases make the atmosphere thicker. As the sun's heat hits the Earth, more and more of the heat is trapped and warms the Earth. As CO_2 increases, so does the temperature. This shows that there is a **link** between CO_2 and temperature. This connection is **evidence** that climate change is caused by humans.

SIGNS OF CLIMATE CHANGE

More **energetic** weather

Increasing drought

Rising sea levels and floods

Can we **adapt** to these changes?

2 Choose the best definition for each word or phrase.

_____ 1. escape

    a. to get out

    b. to change

_____ 2. atmosphere

    a. mixture of gases that surround the Earth

    b. half of a sphere

_____ 3. fossil fuels

    a. substances that are buried in the ground and can be burned for power

    b. solar energy

_____ 4. carbon dioxide (CO_2)

    a. colorless gas breathed out by people and animals

    b. gas we use in our cars

_____ 5. gases

    a. hot air

    b. air-like substances

_____ 6. emissions

    a. sending out of something

    b. representatives

_____ 7. link

    a. effect

    b. connection holding two things together

_____ 8. evidence

    a. interest in something

    b. information that proves something

_____ 9. energetic

    a. visible

    b. powerful

_____ **10. adapt**

      a. to change something to be more useful

      b. to move something

GO TO MyEnglishLab *FOR MORE VOCABULARY PRACTICE.*

PREVIEW

The following article comes from a New Zealand government brochure. Read the title and the subtitles. Why do you think the New Zealand government made this brochure? Check (✓) one of the answers.

_____ **a.** To explain what causes climate change

_____ **b.** To get people to change their lifestyle

_____ **c.** To warn us about the effects of climate change

Now read the article.

Our Climate Is Changing and It Is Going to Keep Changing

Climate Change

1   It's getting hotter. Our climate is changing, so you need to get used to it. It's changing because of what we humans do and the **gases** we have put into the **atmosphere**. We have already put so much gas into the atmosphere, the climate will keep changing for a long, long time. Some of the changes may be good (at least in the short term) and some may be bad. But change is coming.

2   We have known for 30 years that the atmosphere was changing. We knew because there was an increase in **carbon dioxide** (CO_2), the gas we breathe out and the gas produced when we burn **fossil fuels** such as coal and gasoline. This is the same gas that is used by plants to make food. Before 1900 the amount of carbon dioxide in the atmosphere was 270 to 280 parts per million (ppm). Now it has grown to 394 parts per million. At the same time that carbon dioxide was increasing, something else was happening. The world was becoming hotter. It is this **link**, this connection between an increase in carbon dioxide and an increase in temperature, that tells us that carbon dioxide is causing the warming. This **evidence** is proof that humans, in addition to nature, are causing climate change.

(continued on next page)

Not Just Hotter

3   Since the atmosphere is getting hotter, it is also getting more **energetic**. This means that in some places it will be windier, in some places wetter, in some places drier. In some places it may even be cooler. That's why we talk about "climate change" rather than "global warming." Although on average it will be warmer, it won't be warmer everywhere.

Can We Stop It?

4   No. We can slow it, but we can't stop it for a long, long time. We have already made the greenhouse gas **emissions** that will keep the atmosphere changing for decades to come. Even if we could stop the world's greenhouse gas emissions from growing, the temperature would keep growing as fast as it is growing now. If we could reduce emissions by 50 percent, the world would still keep getting hotter for a hundred years or more. But if we act soon, we can make sure the changes can be managed and kept to a minimum, and we can **adapt** to them.

The Greenhouse Gases

5   Our activities make gases that cause climate change; important gases are carbon dioxide, methane, and nitrous oxide. We call these gases "greenhouse gases" because they warm the atmosphere like a greenhouse keeps plants warm. Carbon dioxide is released when we burn fossil fuels like coal and gasoline. Carbon dioxide has a bigger effect than all the other gases put together. Consequently, it is very important to decrease carbon dioxide. All these gases—the ones we produce, and the water vapor in the atmosphere— warm the Earth because they let the sun's heat come in but stop some of the heat from **escaping** out to space.

The Bottom Line

6   The climate is changing and is going to keep changing. Almost every country wants to reduce its emissions. If all the countries of the world act, and act soon, the problems of climate change can be reduced.

Read also this short article about some possible results of climate change.

Some Predictions and Results of Climate Change

Most of the world's land is north of the equator, the middle of the Earth. The farther north you go, the warmer and drier it will become. For example, Siberia has always been harsh and cold, but climate change could cause it to become temperate (not too warm and not too cold). Then it could be an attractive place to take a vacation. Since the soil of Siberia has never been farmed because it was always covered by snow, it would probably be excellent for farming. Agriculture and tourism could make Russia richer than any other country in the world. In contrast, Pakistan may become too hot for its inhabitants. Temperatures in the Punjab are often over 100°F now, but what if climate change causes the temperature to stay above 120 or 130°F? Another example is the Qori Kalis glacier in Peru. As it melts, it has caused flooding in the valley. So now the valley often has too much water. Eventually, however, the glacier will disappear. When it does, the people in the valley will not have enough water and it will be drier. Finally, Western Europe could experience much colder temperatures as a result of changing ocean temperatures.

Now read the information and the chart about CO_2 emissions.

WORLD EMITTERS[1] OF CARBON DIOXIDE

In order to understand how big the problem of gas emissions is, it's helpful to look at how much is being produced and which countries are the biggest producers. The chart below shows how many metric tons of carbon dioxide emissions were being produced by the top 15 emitters in 2008.

TOP 15 EMITTERS OF CARBON DIOXIDE

Rank	Country	Annual CO_2 emissions (in thousands of metric tons[2])	Percentage of total emissions
1	China	7,032,000	23.5%
2	United States	5,461,000	18.3%
3	European Union	4,178,000	14.0%
4	India	1,743,000	5.8%
5	Russia	1,709,000	5.7%
6	Japan	1,208,000	4.0%
7	Germany	787,000	2.6%
8	Canada	544,000	1.8%
9	Iran	538,000	1.8%
10	United Kingdom	523,000	1.8%
11	South Korea	509,000	1.7%
12	Mexico	476,000	1.6%
13	Italy	445,000	1.5%
14	South Africa	436,000	1.5%
15	Saudi Arabia	434,000	1.5%

Source: Wikipedia, 2007 (www.en.wikipedia.org)

Note that New Zealand is not in this group of top emitters of carbon dioxide. In fact, in 2008, New Zealand was ranked as the 73rd emitter, with only 0.1% of emissions.

---

[1] **emitters:** countries that make emissions
[2] **metric ton:** unit for measuring weight, equal to 1,000 kilograms or about 2,205 pounds

MAIN IDEAS

1 Look again at the Preview on page 181. How did your answer help you understand the article?

2 Write **T** (true) or **F** (false) for each statement. Rewrite the false statements to make them true. Share your answers with the class.

　　　　　　　　　　　　　　　　　　　　　　　　　global warming

___F___ **1.** The increase in carbon dioxide is related to ~~our temperature changes~~.

_____ **2.** All places on Earth are getting warmer.

_____ **3.** We can stop global warming if we act now.

_____ **4.** Human activity contributes to the warming of the Earth.

DETAILS

Match the beginning of each sentence on the left with the best ending on the right. There may be more than one correct answer.

_c, f, h_ **1.** Our climate is changing because . . .

_____ **2.** An increase in CO2 showed . . .

_____ **3.** If we could reduce greenhouse gases by 50 percent, . . .

_____ **4.** The largest emitters of CO_2 are . . .

_____ **5.** We know that . . .

_____ **6.** Water vapor and greenhouse gases warm the Earth because . . .

_____ **7.** Since 1900, . . .

_____ **8.** Greenhouse gases are released into the atmosphere when . . .

_____ **9.** It will be warmer on average, but . . .

a. China, the U.S., and the European Union.

b. they allow the heat of the sun in but stop some of the heat from escaping.

c. we burn coal and gasoline.

d. that our atmosphere was changing.

e. it won't be warmer everywhere.

f. the amount of CO_2 in the atmosphere has increased.

g. the atmosphere is getting more energetic.

h. humans have put a lot of gases into the atmosphere.

i. the world would continue heating for about another 100 years.

MAKE INFERENCES

INFERRING PURPOSE

An **inference** is an **educated guess** about something that is **not directly stated** in a text. A strong **reader can understand the writer's purpose** even though the writer does not say it directly.

> Look at the example and read the explanation.

- "Before 1900 the amount of carbon dioxide in the atmosphere was 270 to 280 parts per million (ppm). Now it has grown to 394 parts per million."

What is the purpose of this text?
a. To warn the reader about climate change
b. To make comparisons by looking at two or more things to see how they are similar or different
c. To educate the reader about climate change
(*The best answer is* **c.**)

The text **teaches** us **facts** about greenhouse gases and climate change. The reader learns how the Earth gets warmer.

After reading the text closely, we can **infer** that the **purpose** of the text is **to educate** us about climate change.

> Look at another example and read the explanation.

- Signs of Climate Change: more energetic weather, increasing drought, rising sea levels and floods

What is the purpose of this text?
a. To warn the reader about climate change
b. To make comparisons by looking at two or more things to see how they are similar or different
c. To educate the reader about climate change
(*The best answer is* **a.**)

The text **warns** us about **situations** brought by climate change that could be **dangerous** and perhaps deadly.

After reading the text closely, we can **infer** that the **purpose** of the text is **to warn** us about climate change.

Reading One has three different types of text. Match each text with its purpose.

Texts

_____ **1.** Our Climate Is Changing and It Is Going to Keep Changing

_____ **2.** Some Predictions and Results of Climate Change

_____ **3.** World Emitters of Carbon Dioxide

Purposes

a. To warn the reader about climate change

b. To make comparisons by looking at two or more things to see how they are similar or different

c. To educate the reader about climate change

Now discuss your answers with a partner. Point out the parts of the text that helped you find the answers.

EXPRESS OPINIONS

Work in groups of three. Choose one of the questions. Discuss your ideas. Then choose one person in your group to report the ideas to the class.

1. Some of the climate changes may be good (at least in the short term) and some may be bad. What do you think the good and bad changes will be?

2. The text says: "If we could cut emissions by half, the world would still keep getting hotter for a hundred years or more. But if we act soon, we can make sure the changes can be managed and kept to a minimum, and we can adapt to them." In your opinion, what changes should be made immediately?

3. Look at the World Emitters chart. Is your country on the chart? If so, is it near the top, around the middle, or near the bottom? If not, where do you think it would be? How much does your country contribute to this problem?

▪▪▪▪▪▪▪▪▪▪▪▪▪▪▪▪▪▪▪▪▪▪▪▪▪▪▪ *GO TO* MyEnglishLab *TO GIVE YOUR OPINION ABOUT ANOTHER QUESTION.*

READING TWO CLIMATE CHANGE: MAKING INFORMED DECISIONS

READ

1 Look at the boldfaced words and phrases in the reading and think about the questions.

1. Which words or phrases do you know the meanings of?

2. Can you use any of the words or phrases in a sentence?

CLIMATE CHANGE:
Making Informed[1] Decisions

1   For the past decade, there have been angry **debates** about whether our planet is heating up and whose fault it is. Scientists, politicians, journalists, and famous entertainers are all saying that our planet is in trouble and that human beings are the cause. They say we must act now to reduce our use of fossil fuels before it is too late. At the same time, a few governments and some scientists argue there is no evidence that humans are causing recent changes in climate and weather. Clearly, the experts can't agree. So, what is the average person supposed to think, or do, about this issue?

2   *Can carbon dioxide produced by humans cause climate change?* This question was first studied in the early 1900s. For the next 60 years, most scientists did not think that the daily actions or lifestyles of humans could really change the Earth's temperature. Since then, however, many scientists have thought that our actions *do* make a difference. In 1988, a group of scientists called the International Panel on Climate Change (IPCC) met to discuss three important issues: 1) how our lifestyles **affect** the Earth's climate, 2) how climate change would affect us in the future, and 3) how to deal with climate change. Later, the IPCC ideas were used to write the Kyoto Protocol, a 1997 agreement that explained our role in the Earth's changing atmosphere and set international **limits** for gas emissions from 2008–2012. Some countries have decided to continue these reductions until 2020. However, CO_2 emissions are now more than 50 percent higher than in 1990.

3   A few governments, including the United States and Saudi Arabia, and some companies don't support the Kyoto Protocol. They think achieving the limits that were put in the Protocol would cost too much money and be bad for business. Scientists who work for these governments and companies argue that recent climate change is not actually caused by humans. These scientists don't think we really need to change our lifestyles; that is, we should continue to drive, fly, and live normally. They present evidence that proves that the Earth is going through a normal heating and cooling cycle, as it has done throughout its history.

4   So, is there a link between humans and climate change or not? Who should we believe? The IPCC or the governments and companies that disagree with it? To reach an educated opinion, it is important to think about the people who make scientific claims and what their purposes may be. For example, some say the scientists who **warn** about global warming are trying to scare people in order to get attention and money for their research. According to Petr Chylek, Professor of Physics and Atmospheric Sciences at Dalhousie University in Nova Scotia, scientists can only get this attention and money "by making things bigger and more dangerous than they really are."

5   And what about the other experts who say our use of fossil fuels is *not* causing climate change? Well, some of *them* get money from companies that produce these fossil fuels. For example, ExxonMobil, one of the world's

---

[1] **informed:** involving a lot of knowledge or information

biggest oil companies, has spent millions of dollars to support groups that discredit[2] the idea of global warming. Two groups have criticized ExxonMobil for this. One is the Union of Concerned Scientists, a group of watchdog[3] scientists in the United States. Another is the Royal Society, Britain's top scientific academy. Both groups have said ExxonMobil is trying to confuse people with incorrect and dishonest information about climate change.

6   Clearly, scientific information can be affected by the interests of individual scientists. When we hear reports on climate change, we must use good judgment and ask ourselves where the facts are coming from. We must interpret the research, make informed decisions, and most importantly, participate in the debate.

---

[2] **discredit:** to criticize someone or something so that they are not respected

[3] **watchdog:** a person or group that makes sure other people follow rules

COMPREHENSION

Answer the questions.

1. Whose recommendations were used to write the Kyoto Protocol?

_____

2. What limits were set by the Kyoto Protocol?

_____

3. Why does Petr Chylek say scientists want to make things seem more dangerous than they are?

_____

4. Why has ExxonMobil spent millions of dollars?

_____

5. Why do the Union of Concerned Scientists and the Royal Society criticize ExxonMobil?

_____

GO TO MyEnglishLab FOR MORE VOCABULARY PRACTICE.

READING SKILL

1 Read this quote from Reading Two. Then answer the question.

"For the next 60 years, most scientists did not think that the daily actions or lifestyles of humans could really change the Earth's temperature. Since then, however, many scientists have thought that our actions *do* make a difference." *(paragraph 2)*

What information follows the word **however**? What information comes before it?

IDENTIFYING COHESIVE DEVICES OF CONTRAST

Writers use **cohesive devices of contrast** to **introduce opposing ideas** in a text. A cohesive device of contrast is a **word or phrase** that tells us that the information that will follow is different from what comes before it.

Look at the example again and read the explanation.

- "For the next 60 years, most scientists did not think that the daily actions or lifestyles of humans could really change the Earth's temperature. Since then, ***however,*** many scientists have thought that our actions *do* make a difference."

In the first sentence, most scientists **did not think** that our actions or lifestyles could really change the Earth's temperature. In the second sentence, many scientists do **think** that our actions make a difference.

The use of the word ***however*** helps the reader to **expect contrast** (different information), NOT comparison (similar information). ***However*** is a **cohesive device of contrast**.

---

2 Work with a partner. Read the quotes from Reading One ("Some Predictions and Results of Climate Change"). Which words are cohesive devices to show contrast? What do they contrast?

1. "Agriculture and tourism could make Russia richer than any other country in the world. In contrast, Pakistan may become too hot for its inhabitants."

2. "Temperatures in the Punjab are often over 100°F now, but what if climate change causes the temperature to stay above 120 or 130°F?"

3. "So now the valley often has too much water. Eventually, however, the glacier will disappear."

⬛⬛⬛⬛⬛⬛⬛⬛⬛⬛⬛⬛⬛⬛⬛⬛⬛⬛⬛⬛⬛⬛⬛⬛ *GO TO* MyEnglishLab *FOR MORE SKILL PRACTICE.*

STEP 1: Organize

A causal chain helps you to see the relationships between causes and effects. Look at the causal chain below describing the information in Reading One and Reading Two. The green indicates information from Reading One; the purple indicates information from Reading Two. Look back at the readings to fill in the missing causes and effects from the choices below.

   a. The Kyoto Protocol is signed

   b. Some gases stay in the atmosphere

   c. Companies such as ExxonMobil hire scientists to discredit other scientists

   d. Fossil fuels (coal and gasoline) are burned

   e. The atmosphere gets more energetic

   f. Some gases get used by plants to make food

ExxonMobil produces fossil fuels → (1) _Fossil fules (coal and gasoline) are burned._ → Greenhouse gases are put into the atmosphere. → (2) _____

→ (3) _____

→ The atmosphere gets warmer. → (4) _____ → Climate change → The IPCC meets to discuss climate change issues. →

→ (5) _____ → The Kyoto Protocol sets international limits for gas emissions. → (6) _____

Complete a summary of the cause-and-effect relationships of ExxonMobil, scientists, and climate change. Use information from Step 1.

There is an interesting relationship between oil companies, scientists, and climate change.

ExxonMobil is a company that produces fossil fuels. *When fossil fuels such as coal and* ___

gasoline are burned, greenhouse gases are put into the atmosphere. ___

___

___

___

___

As the climate began to change, a group of scientists called the International Panel on

Climate Change (IPCC) began to study the effects of climate change.

___

___

___

___

Hopefully, we will be able to slow climate change by using less of the fossil fuels in the future.

GO TO MyEnglishLab TO CHECK WHAT YOU LEARNED.

VOCABULARY

REVIEW

Read the story about a group called the Global Climate Coalition. Complete the story with the words from the box.

adapt	debate	evidence	link
affecting	~~emissions~~	fossil fuels	warned
atmosphere	energetic	gases	
carbon dioxide	escaped	limits	

The Global Climate Coalition

The Global Climate Coalition (GCC) was founded in 1987. It was a group that included some

of the most powerful oil companies. Among its members were British Petroleum (BP), Royal

Dutch Shell, Dupont,, and the Ford Motor Company. In 1997, just before the Kyoto Conference

on Climate Change, it started a massive advertising campaign. The purpose of this campaign was

to stop the United States from agreeing to reduce gas _____emissions_____ . The ads tried to
　　　　　　　　　　　　　　　　　　　　　　　　　　　1.

frighten Americans. They _____ Americans that if they set _____
　　　　　　　　　　　　　　　2.　　　　　　　　　　　　　　　　　　　　　　　　3.

for the use of _____, the price of gasoline would go up 50 cents a gallon. This
　　　　　　　　4.

wasn't true, but the campaign was successful.

Even though the public image of the GCC was good, there were problems. The chairman

of BP announced in May 1997 that the _____ between greenhouse
　　　　　　　　　　　　　　　　　　　　　5.

_____ and climate change was too strong to ignore. BP left the Global Climate
　　6.

Coalition. Dupont and Royal Dutch Shell also left. In 1999, Ford _____ from the
　　　　　　　　　　　　　　　　　　　　　　　　　　　　　　　　　　7.

GCC. Ford's decision showed that fossil fuel industries were changing. In 2000, DaimlerChrysler,

Texaco, and General Motors left the Coalition, too. Leading companies left the Global Climate

Coalition because there was more and more _____ that the _____
　　　　　　　　　　　　　　　　　　　　　　　8.　　　　　　　　　　　　　9.

(continued on next page)

was really getting warmer and more _____, and that _____ was
                                                    10.   11.
the cause. The GCC represented old thinking, while the companies leaving were the companies

trying to _____ to the new information about climate change science. These
                          12.
companies joined a new group called the Business Environmental Leadership Council, as did

Toyota and Boeing. Companies that joined the Council had to have their own programs to reduce

carbon emissions.

    The GCC closed in 2002. The organization which successfully stopped the United States from

agreeing to the Kyoto Protocol in 1997 has stopped _____ the global climate
                                                                              13.
_____.
            14.

EXPAND

Look at the list of nouns taken from Reading One and Reading Two. Which of these nouns
can be used with the adjectives below? Some nouns can be used more than once.

agreement	coal	emissions	government
atmosphere	confusion	evidence	limits
carbon dioxide	debate	fossil fuels	production
climate	doubt	gas	public

   1. successful: _____ *agreement, government, production* _____

   2. clear: _____

   3. warm: _____

4. powerful: _____

5. energetic: _____

6. harmful: _____

7. increasing: _____

8. national: _____

9. educated: _____

10. massive: _____

CREATE

Write a paragraph explaining different views of climate change science. Use at least five of these words.

affect	climate	emissions	government	public
agreement	confusion	evidence	limits	purpose
atmosphere	debate	fossil fuels	production	warn
carbon dioxide	doubt	gas		

GO TO MyEnglishLab FOR MORE VOCABULARY PRACTICE.

GRAMMAR

1 Read the paragraph. Underline the words **may, might,** and **could**.

Computers are used to make models of how the climate might respond to more carbon dioxide in the atmosphere. Some of the changes may be good, and some may be bad. Since the atmosphere is getting more energetic, some places will be warmer, some places will be wetter, and some places will be drier. Some places may even be cooler. Many of the changes will cause shortages of drinking water and food for people and animals, especially poor people. But if we could cut emissions by half, we could manage the changes and adapt to them.

FUTURE POSSIBILITY: *MAY, MIGHT, COULD*

1. Use *may, might,* and *could* to talk about **future possibility**.	It **may** be windier. It **might** be drier. It **could** be managed.
2. Use *may not* and *might not* to express the possibility that something will not happen. Use *couldn't* to express the idea that something is impossible. **BE CAREFUL!** We usually do not contract *might not,* and we never contract *may not*.	There are a lot of clouds, but it **might not rain**. We **couldn't** stop carbon dioxide emissions completely, but we could reduce them. USE: If we develop new fuels, we **may not need** oil in the future. NOT: If we develop new fuels, we ~~mayn't~~ need oil in the future.
3. Questions about possibility usually do not use *may, might,* or *could*. Instead, they use the future (*will, be going to*), the present progressive, or phrases such as *Do you think . . . ?* or *Is it possible that . . . ?* The **answers** to these questions often use *may, might,* or *could*. In **short answers** to yes/no questions, use *may, might,* or *could* alone. **USAGE NOTE:** If *be* is the main verb, it is common to include *be* in the short answer.	Q: When **will** CO$_2$ levels **come down**? A: They **might start** coming down in 100 years. Q: **Are** we **going to be able** to adapt? A: We **might adapt** if we limit emissions soon. Q: When **will** the temperature **stop rising**? A: It **may stop** in 100 years. Q: **Do you think** developing countries **will reduce** gas emissions? A: They **could reduce** them if it's not too expensive. Q: Is ExxonMobil going to continue to discredit global warming? A: It **might**. Q: Will emissions **be reduced** quickly? A: They **might be**.

2 Complete the questions and answers to express future possibility. There may be more than one correct answer.

1. Q: How much are sea levels going to rise in the next 100 years?

    A: Sea levels <u>_may / might/ /could_</u> rise from seven inches to two feet.

2. Q: What will the weather be like in Siberia?

    A: It _____ be warm and comfortable.

3. Q: Will some places be wetter?

    A: They _____ be.

4. Q: When will sea levels stop rising?

   A: They _____ stop rising in 100 years.

5. Q: _____ coastal areas flood?

   A: They might.

6. Q: _____ some places _____ colder?

   A: They might be.

7. Q: How much stronger do you think hurricanes could get?

   A: They _____ get up to Category 5½.

3 Work with a partner. Make questions about climate change in your country or a country that you're interested in. Share your questions with the class.

▪▪▪▪▪▪▪▪▪▪▪▪▪▪▪▪▪▪▪▪▪▪▪▪▪▪▪▪▪▪▪▪▪▪▪▪▪ *GO TO* MyEnglishLab *TO CHECK WHAT YOU LEARNED.*

FINAL WRITING TASK

In this unit, you read a brochure and an editorial about climate change.

Now you are going to **write an essay about how climate change is affecting your home country or another country**. What changes have already occurred? What is changing now? What changes are predicted for the future? Explain the causes and effects of these changes. Use the vocabulary and grammar from the unit.*

PREPARE TO WRITE: Using a Causal Chain

1 Look at the causal chain. A causal chain helps you to see the relationships between causes and effects. The arrows show how one or more causes leads to one or more effects.

_____ → _____ → _____ → _____ →

_____ → _____ → _____ → _____

2 Think of the causes and effects you will be writing about. Draw a causal chain to help you organize the cause-and-effect relationships.

---

* For Alternative Writing Topics, see page 203. These topics can be used in place of the writing topic for this unit or as homework. The alternative topics relate to the theme of the unit but may not target the same grammar or rhetorical structures taught in the unit.

In a **cause-and-effect essay**, you explain the **relationships** between the causes and effects of a situation. Often, there are many causes which result in one effect or one cause which results in many effects.

1 Read the essay and complete the activities that follow.

1   The future of climate change does not look very good for our Earth. There will be flooding of coastlines, water shortages, and food shortages. The areas near the middle of the world will suffer the most because they will become hotter and experience more storms and dry weather. The poor will become poorer and the wealthy will become wealthier. Africa will experience the worst effects of climate change due to irregular weather, the rising temperature of the atmosphere and water, and rising sea levels.

2   Africa's climates have always been irregular, and now climate change is causing more irregular weather. Dry areas are becoming drier and wet areas are becoming wetter. In the future, this will hurt people who grow their own food since the time of the growing season and the amount of food they get will decrease. Since 70 percent of Africa's people grow their own food, they will not have enough. In some countries, the amount of food grown could decrease by 50 percent.

3   Another problem is the rising temperature of the atmosphere and water. Africa is an average 0.5°F hotter than it was 100 years ago. In some areas, however, it is as much as 3.5°F hotter, and it is believed that it will be 7–9°F hotter in the next 100 years. As a result, the earth in Africa is becoming drier. Another result is that the glaciers are melting. The snows of Kilimanjaro are expected to disappear in the next 10–20 years. Also, rising water temperatures in lakes will result in fewer fish, another important food. In addition, the rising temperature of the North Atlantic will cause rain to occur further and further north, so that northern Africa will experience less and less rain. This will cause more drought. Consequently, by 2020, 75–250 million people in Africa will not have enough water.

(continued on next page)

4   In the next 50 to 100 years, there will be flooding of coastlines since sea levels will rise. Many people live along the coastlines of Africa, and these people will become homeless. They will have to move away from the coastline. For most of them, there will be little help from the government. In addition, some of the best farmland will be under water. This will result in more food shortages.

5   The latest studies of climate change show that Africa may be in a more dangerous situation than any other continent. According to Andrew Simms of the New Economics Foundation, "Global warming is set to make many of the problems which Africa already deals with much, much worse." Unless the rich countries of the world reduce gas emissions now, we will see millions of Africans die of hunger and sickness.

1. Read the introductory paragraph. What is the thesis statement (main idea of the essay)? Underline it.

2. Read paragraph 2 and draw a cause-and-effect map for it.

3. Read paragraph 3 and draw a cause-and-effect map for it.

4. Read paragraph 4 and draw a cause-and-effect map for it.

2 Look back at the causal chain you wrote in Prepare to Write, page 196. Add notes about reasons, examples, and facts to support your causes and effects.

3 Use your causal chain and notes to write the first draft of your cause-and-effect essay. It will have the following:

- **An introductory paragraph** including a thesis statement (main idea of your essay) about how climate change is affecting the country of your choice

- **Three body paragraphs**, each one focusing on one set of cause-and-effect relationships; each body paragraph will give reasons, examples, and facts to support your causes and effects

- **A concluding paragraph** summarizing your main ideas or restating the thesis statement and adding a final comment

1 Look at the sentences taken from Reading One. What do the boldfaced words mean?

- All these gases—the ones we produce, and the water vapor in the atmosphere—warm the Earth **because** they let the sun's heat come in but stop some of the heat from escaping out to space.

- **Since** the atmosphere is getting hotter, it is also getting more energetic.

- Carbon dioxide has a bigger total effect than all the other gases put together. **Consequently**, it is very important to decrease carbon dioxide.

- We have already made the greenhouse gas emissions that will keep the atmosphere changing for decades to come. **Therefore**, even if we stop the emissions now, the Earth will continue to warm.

Because, since, consequently, and *therefore* are **transitions**. Writers use transitions to help the reader move from one idea to the next. These words or phrases prepare the reader for what type of information will come next.

Because and *since* show **cause**. *Consequently* and *therefore* show **effect**.

2 Read the information about cause-and-effect transitions.

Different transitions are used to show **cause and effect**. Transitions used to show **cause** are also called **adverbial conjunctions**. Notice that these transitions are used with a complete sentence containing a subject and verb.

ADVERBIAL CONJUNCTIONS USED TO SHOW CAUSE

because   since   as
- It's changing **because** humans have put gases into the atmosphere.
- In the next 50 to 100 years, there will be flooding of coastlines **since** sea levels will rise.
- We know that the atmosphere is getting more energetic **as** it is getting hotter.

TRANSITIONS USED TO SHOW EFFECT

Therefore,   Consequently,   Thus,   As a result,
- **Therefore**, ExxonMobil thought of a good way to avoid this problem.
- **Consequently**, it has only one goal: to make money by selling fossil fuels.
- The atmosphere is getting hotter and more energetic. **Thus**, in some places it will be windier, in some places wetter, in some places drier.
- The climate is changing. **As a result**, every country in the world will be affected.

3 Read this report about climate change around the world. Complete the sentences with the best choice of transitions. You may need to add commas to some sentences.

According to the IPCC, climate change in the next century could bring both benefits and problems to different parts of the world. In Africa, up to 400 million people will not have enough water. _____*Since*_____ this will hurt agriculture, or farming, there will not be enough
      1. (Since / As a result,)
food. _____ more people in Africa will be malnourished. The water
      2. (As a result, / Because)
temperature of lakes will increase. _____ there will be less and less fish to
      3. (Consequently, / As)
eat.

In Asia, the melting of glaciers will first cause flooding. Later, _____
      4. (therefore, / as)
the glaciers get smaller, the rivers will dry up. In some areas of Asia, agriculture will improve 20 percent, while in other areas it will decrease by 30 percent.

There will be less rain in Australia and New Zealand. _____ there will be
      5. (As a result, / Since)
less water and less clean water. In southern and eastern Australia there will be drought and fires. In some areas of New Zealand, however, farming will improve because it will be warmer and there will be more rain. _____ the coastal areas will have more and bigger
      6. (Because / Consequently,)
storms, there will be more flooding.

In northern Europe, it will be warmer. _____ agriculture will
      7. (Therefore, / As)
increase and forests will grow. In southern Europe, there will be drought and water shortages
_____ it will be warmer.
      8. (therefore, / since)
In North America, it will be warmer and drier. _____ there will be more
      9. (As a result, / As)
fires and disease, and problems with insects. _____ some areas will be drier,
      10. (Because / Thus,)
Latin America will have a decrease in agriculture. _____ sea temperature
      11. (As a result, / As)
will rise, there will be fewer fish in some places. These things will result in food shortages.

4 Go back to the first draft of your essay. Add cause-and-effect transitions to help the reader move from one idea to the next. Don't forget to use commas where needed.

GO TO MyEnglishLab FOR MORE SKILL PRACTICE.

EDIT: Writing the Final Draft

Go to MyEnglishLab and write the final draft of your essay. Carefully edit it for grammatical and mechanical errors, such as spelling, capitalization, and punctuation. Make sure you use some of the vocabulary and grammar from the unit. Use the checklist to help you write your final draft. Then submit your essay to your teacher.

FINAL DRAFT CHECKLIST

❑ Does your essay clearly explain the causes and effects that you think are important for your topic?

❑ Does it contain an introductory paragraph, three body paragraphs, and a concluding paragraph?

❑ Does the introductory paragraph contain a thesis statement stating the main idea of your essay?

❑ Does each body paragraph focus on one set of cause-and-effect relationships?

❑ Does each body paragraph contain reasons, examples, and facts to support the causes and effects?

❑ Do you use cause-and-effect transitions to help the reader move from one idea to the next?

❑ Does the concluding paragraph restate the main idea expressed in the thesis statement?

❑ Do you use *may, might,* or *could* to express future possibility?

❑ Do you use new vocabulary from the unit?

UNIT PROJECT

Work in a small group. Investigate one aspect of the climate change problem. Write a report about your findings. Follow these steps:

STEP 1: Research online one of these aspects of climate change science:

- The "hockey stick"
- Cylinders of ice cores taken from glaciers
- Measurements of CO_2 in the atmosphere
- The ocean's temperatures, especially in the North Atlantic
- Melting glaciers
- The increase in frequency and strength of storms
- Rising sea levels
- Migrations of species
- The Kyoto Protocol
- The International Panel on Climate Change
- Collapsing ice shelves in Antarctica
- Effects of volcanic eruptions on the atmosphere

STEP 2: Answer these questions about the topic you have chosen:

- Who is responsible for initiating this study?
- How long have people been studying this?
- Why is this information important?
- How will this information help us in the future?
- Is this a major or minor part of climate change?

STEP 3: Use your notes from Step 2 to write a report (three or four paragraphs). Prepare a visual aid for your report. Share your report with the class.

ALTERNATIVE WRITING TOPICS

Write about one of the topics. Use the vocabulary and grammar from the unit.

1. Think about how your life will change in 20 years as a result of climate change. Write an essay discussing the positive and negative changes in your life.

2. Imagine you work for a government organization that provides help to victims of disasters. Write a report (three or four paragraphs) about a natural disaster that you know about. What caused the disaster? What were the results of the disaster? Who helped the victims after it happened? Did the government provide most of the help (relief)? Did international organizations help? How long did it take for this area to recover?

3. Do you think you can do anything personally to slow down climate change? If so, what? How much action are you willing to take? What do you think you will achieve? Write a journal entry (three or four paragraphs) about your reaction to information about climate change.

■■■■■■■■■■■■■■■■■■■■■■■■■■■■■■■ GO TO MyEnglishLab TO WRITE ABOUT ONE OF THE ALTERNATIVE TOPICS, WATCH A VIDEO ABOUT A FAMILY LIVING THE SIMPLE LIFE, AND TAKE THE UNIT 8 ACHIEVEMENT TEST. ■■■

GRAMMAR BOOK REFERENCES

NorthStar: Reading and Writing Level 3, Fourth Edition	Focus on Grammar Level 3, Fourth Edition	Azar's Fundamentals of English Grammar, Fourth Edition
Unit 1 Ability: *Can, Could, Be able to*	**Unit 13** Ability: *can, could, be able to*	**Chapter 7** Modal Auxiliaries: 7-2
Unit 2 Simple Past and Past Progressive	**Unit 3** Past Progressive and Simple Past	**Chapter 2** Past Time: 2-6
Unit 3 Infinitives of Purpose	**Unit 25** More Uses of Infinitives	**Chapter 13** Gerunds and Infinitives: 13-4
Unit 4 Comparative Adverbs	**Unit 22** Adverbs: As . . . as, Comparatives, Superlatives	**Chapter 9** Comparisons: 9-3
Unit 5 Future Time Clauses	**Unit 7** Future Time Clauses	**Chapter 3** Future Time: 3-6
Unit 6 *Because* and *Even though*	Part IX From Grammar to Writing Combining Sentences with *Because, Although, Even though*	**Chapter 8** Connecting Ideas: 8-6, 8-7
Unit 7 Definite and Indefinite Articles	**Unit 18** Articles: Indefinitive and Definite	**Chapter 11** Count/Noncount Nouns and Articles: 11-8
Unit 8 Future Possibility: *May, Might, Could*	**Unit 31** Future Possibility: *May, Might, Could*	**Chapter 7** Modal Auxiliaries 7-3, 7-4

UNIT WORD LIST

The Unit Word List is a summary of key vocabulary from the Student Book.
Words followed by an asterisk (*) are on the Academic Word List (AWL).

UNIT 1

accomplished (adj.)
challenge (n.)*
complications
daring (n.)
do-or-die (adj.)
enormous*

focused*
impressive
inspire
obsession
pressure (n.)
risk (n.)
unthinkable
willingness

UNIT 2

astonishing
con man/woman
deception
duplicate (adj.)
fake (adj.)
fishy

fraud
honesty
impersonate
motive*
suspicious
weary

UNIT 3

artificial
automatically*
boredom
count on
depression*
engine
establish*

isolated*
reaction*
research (n.)*
simulate*
speculation
spin (v.)
survive*

UNIT 4

assertive
dialect
dominate*
exception
excessive
inferior
myth
profanity

proverb
sexism*
slang
synonym
talkative
uniqueness*
valued (adj.)

UNIT 5

benefit (n.)*
ensure*
entrepreneur
expert*
freelancer
injured*

obsolete
outsource (v.)
prospects (n.)*
security*
strategy*
sustainable*

UNIT 6

coastal
consequence*
continent (n.)
environment*
fragile
frozen
harsh
inhabit

landscape (n.)
preserve (v.)
protect
remote (adj.)
research
tourist
vast

UNIT 7

arranged marriage
background
characteristics
everlasting
fertility
leadership
monogamy

polygamy
pregnant
produce (v.)
raise
romantic
shocked
spouse

UNIT 8

adapt*
affect (v.)*
atmosphere
carbon dioxide
debate (n.)*
emissions
energetic*

escape (v.)
evidence*
fossil fuels
gases
limits
link (n.)*
warn

TEXT CREDITS

UNIT 2
THE ART OF THE STEAL: HOW TO PROTECT YOURSELF AND YOUR BUSINESS FROM FRAUD—AMERICA'S #1 CRIME by Frank W. Abagnale, Jr., copyright © 2001 by Frank W. Abagnale. Used by permission of Broadway Books, a division of Random House, Inc. Any third party use of this material, outside of this publication, is prohibited. Interested parties must apply directly to Random House, Inc. for permission.

UNIT 5
What is a 21st Century Career? Southern New Hampshire University.

UNIT 8
"Our Climate is Changing and It is Going to Keep Changing Adapted" from *Gentle Footprints Boots 'n All,* a New Zealand Government publications. www.mfe.govt.nz/publications/ser/gentle-footprints-May06. May 16, 2007. Reprinted with the permission of the Ministry for the Environment, New Zealand.

PHOTO CREDITS

Cover photo credits: (top left) Hill Street Studios/Blend Images/Corbis, (top right) a1center/Fotolia, (middle left) monika3steps/Shutterstock, (middle right) a1center/Fotolia, (bottom left) Comstock Images/Getty Images, (bottom right) Lou Linwei/Alamy.

Page xii (top) ABC News; p. 2 EpicStockMedia/Fotolia; p. 5 Aurora Photos/Alamy; p. 15 Everett Collection Inc/Alamy; p. 24 davidevison/Fotolia; p. 28 Presselect/Alamy; p. 48 NASA/UPI/Newscom; p. 50 JPL-Caltech/MSSS/NASA; p. 52 NASA Images; p. 57 NASA/JPL/NASA Images; p. 74 Phase4Photography/Fotolia; p. 76 Jupiterimages/Photolibrary/Getty Images; p. 84 (left) imagebroker/Alamy, (middle) Eddie Gerald/Alamy, (right) FER737NG/Fotolia; p. 100 Radius Images/Alamy; p. 102 Monkey Business Images/Shutterstock; p. 104 Pixsooz/Fotolia; p. 105 JDC/LWA/Corbis/Glow Images;
p. 110 wavebreakmedia/Shutterstock; p. 128 John Warburton-Lee Photography/Alamy;
p. 132 maurice joseph/Alamy; p. 136 staphy/Fotolia; p. 137 Keren Su/China Span/Alamy;
p. 138 BMJ/Shutterstock; p. 152 Ariadne Van Zandbergen/Alamy; p. 156 Jon Arnold Images Ltd/Alamy; p. 161 Nga Nguyen/Flickr Select/Getty Images; p. 176 a1center/Fotolia;
p. 179 (top) razlomov/Fotolia, (middle) roca83/Fotolia, (bottom) egd/Shutterstock;
p. 181 (left) cobaltstock/Fotolia,(right) David Sprott/Shutterstock; p. 194 Lane Erickson/Fotolia.

THE PHONETIC ALPHABET

Consonant Symbols			
/b/	**b**e	/t/	**t**o
/d/	**d**o	/v/	**v**an
/f/	**f**ather	/w/	**w**ill
/g/	**g**et	/y/	**y**es
/h/	**h**e	/z/	**z**oo, bu**s**y
/k/	**k**eep, **c**an	/θ/	**th**anks
/l/	**l**et	/ð/	**th**en
/m/	**m**ay	/ʃ/	**sh**e
/n/	**n**o	/ʒ/	vi**s**ion, A**s**ia
/p/	**p**en	/tʃ/	**ch**ild
/r/	**r**ain	/dʒ/	**j**oin
/s/	**s**o, **c**ircle	/ŋ/	lo**ng**

Vowel Symbols			
/ɑ/	f**a**r, h**o**t	/iy/	**we**, m**ea**n, f**ee**t
/ɛ/	m**e**t, s**ai**d	/ey/	d**ay**, l**a**te, r**ai**n
/ɔ/	t**a**ll, b**ou**ght	/ow/	g**o**, l**ow**, c**oa**t
/ə/	s**o**n, **u**nder	/uw/	t**oo**, bl**ue**
/æ/	c**a**t	/ay/	t**i**me, b**uy**
/ɪ/	sh**i**p	/aw/	h**ou**se, n**ow**
/ʊ/	g**oo**d, c**ou**ld, p**u**t	/oy/	b**oy**, c**oi**n